Common
Cagebirds
in
America

Common Cagebirds in America

VAL CLEAR

With Photographs by Tommy Wadelton

THE BOBBS-MERRILL COMPANY, INC.
A Subsidiary of Howard W. Sams & Co., Inc. / Publishers
Indianapolis · Kansas City · New York

JUL 19 1966

TO
EVELYN

perpetually patient and understanding
with her
bird-brained husband.

Contents

List of Illustrations

Preface

M OST OF US LIVE in rather artificial environments. We exist in worlds of paperclips and typewriters, of drill presses and calculators, of escalators and glass walls, of TV dinners and electric toothbrushes. Modern technology has not left us much of what used to fill man with joy and satisfaction when he lived close to nature's world, and although we have new gratifications, we long for some of the old ones.

I think that must be why there has been such a fantastic explosion of interest in cagebirds in America. From all over the world we bring birds by the thousands every month, and over twenty million American homes are now made more joyful by the presence of one or more of the species described in this book.

A number of years ago I went to a bird store just a stone's throw from one of the busiest corners in the world, State and Madison Streets in Chicago. Whenever I was in the Loop I always visited that shop to see and hear the birds because I could not keep a pet in our student apartment, and the clerk had come to recognize me as a frequent visitor who never bought a thing. The bird shop was on the third floor, but the noises of the city that Carl Sandburg called "the hog-butcher of the world" assaulted us through the open windows. On that particular day I stood for a long time listening to a roller canary sing his heart out, prancing and almost bursting with the music in his tiny body. The noise of the city came through the window like the background music of a symphony orchestra, and the canary played his part in the impromptu concerto. I was enraptured, dwelling in another world for a few stolen moments. Then the clerk broke the spell by saying to me simply and understandingly, as if she were merely reaffirming a mutually recognized fact, "You know, he can sing the Lord's music even better in your home."

It has been twenty years since that conversation but I recall it often. How many times I have seen a bird bring peace to a troubled mind, companionship to a lonely person, the Lord's music to a painfully empty apartment.

The emptiness of so much of today's living can be made a bit more meaningful by the presence of one of these feathered creatures. It is with the hope that this book may make "the Lord's music" a bit more enjoyable for its readers that it has been written.

No book of this kind is ever written by the author in isolation. It has been over thirty years since I bought my first pair of Zebra Finches, and these decades have multiplied friendships on every continent on the globe while I have pursued the subject in person and in writing. I am indebted to an endless chain of friends and authors.

VAL CLEAR

Anderson, Indiana
February, 1966

Common
Cagebirds
in
America

1

Singers

THE MOST DELIGHTFUL ALARM CLOCK ever invented is a pair of Pekin Robins greeting the earliest streak of dawn with their incomparably rich, warm notes for a new day. We used to have a pair in our living room aviary, and while we had them there, no mechanical alarm was necessary in our nearby bedroom.

Undoubtedly one of the main reasons why people keep birds is the cheer their songs spread. Canaries were domesticated centuries ago for that reason, and through skilled management they have been improved immeasurably over the original Serin from which they were developed.

There are a number of unusually generous singers now being shipped into the United States from abroad. Some of them are quite inexpensive and easily cared for.

Strawberry Finch

The Strawberry Finch (*Amandava amandava*) is probably the commonest of all the singing species now being imported. It is a tiny bird, only a bit larger than our native Ruby-Throated Hummingbird, and for this reason should be kept in a finch cage. The

Strawberry Finches (true pair).

Green Singing Finch (male).

wide spacing on a budgie cage will not hold the Strawberry, and even a canary cage will permit him to squeeze through the bars when frightened.

I do not know of any bird that has quite the lyrical quality of the Strawberry. His song starts high up the scale and then rambles down from the heights in a rather unpremeditated manner, like a falling leaf. He sings often, and although the note is light and thin, it carries well and can be heard throughout the house or neighborhood.

In addition to his musical artistry, the Strawberry also has physical beauty. There are two rather distinct races, one coming from South Central Asia and the other from East Asia. The more commonly imported one comes from India. It is a mahogany-red color rather than the brilliant red that comes from China. Both have small cream spots on their wings and bodies, reminding one of the seeds on a strawberry.

The Strawberry Finch is, I believe, the only member of the waxbill family living outside Africa. It is also the only one to give the male a complete change of color. During the breeding season (our winter in North America) he appears in full sartorial splendor. The male assumes his nuptial plumage and stays in it for several months, after which he becomes a duplicate of the drab female. She never changes color. Thus, when the males are out of color, it is very hard to separate them from the females.

Because of this fact, the clever bird merchants of India have developed a share-the-wealth device that keeps the market in Strawberry Finches alive even in the off-color season. They dip the birds completely in vegetable dye, furnishing them in a full range of bright colors from canary yellow to Kelly green. These are listed on some bird lists as "Painted Finches," but they are not to be confused with two other species that use the same name. If one does not object to beauty that is not even skin deep, these ersatz beauties are indeed colorful. Unfortunately, most people who buy them do not know what they are getting, and they are dismayed after a few weeks to find that their moulting darlings are speckled specimens. It is even worse if they are female, rather colorless brownish creatures.

Strawberry Finches are peaceful around other birds. They thrive on the standard finch diet. For breeding purposes they prefer about a 5-inch-cube nestbox, with the front half open. Although they will create their own nesting material out of paper and feathers, they like short pieces of burlap twine, fine twigs, dry grass, and similar forms of material. They need live food for their babies.

Green Singing Finch and Gray Singing Finch

Two other commonly imported birds noted for their song are the Green Singing Finch (*Serinus mozambicus*) and the Gray Singing

Finch (*Serinus leucopygia*). Both of these come from tropical Africa, and although they are quite similar in most other ways, they do not look at all alike.

The Green Singing Finch is really misnamed. He is yellow and gray, not green. About two-thirds the size of a common canary, his song closely resembles that of the canary. They are close enough genetically that hybrids have often been raised, usually with the hen being a small domestic canary, since it is the hen that has the responsibility of setting and feeding, and a canary is more steady than a finch for these purposes.

The male sings frequently, insistently, and loudly during that part of the year when he is in song. He may become a bit pugnacious at this time, too, and should be watched for the protection of others in the same enclosure. Courtship can become violent, and he may appear to be a vigorous wife-beater, but she seems to like it that way and rarely suffers much from the apparent mayhem.

Sexing the Green Singing Finch can be done with moderate success. The male is brighter in color than the female, but this is complicated a bit by the fact that both sexes get brighter as they get older, so an old hen may be brighter than a young cock. If one is seen singing, it is, of course, a male.

The Greens breed best in a planted aviary. I have never heard of a successful breeding in a cage, although I could readily believe such a report. The species is one that takes very well to cage life, and I should expect it to domesticate nicely.

The Gray Singing Finch is about as naturally tame as any seed-eater I know. My Grays meet me on the front wire of their flights as soon as I enter the birdroom and they stay there to carry on a conversation with me. They seem to have no fear.

And their main mission in life is to make music. They sing, sing, sing, a cheerful, chattery warble that goes on and on. The male usually fluffs the feathers on his head while he sings, and his tiny black eyes glisten like shiny buttons on a pinchushion.

The Gray Singing Finch is very plain colored. He is a soft, brownish gray all over, with occasional light streaks, especially on the breast, and white lower underparts. There is little to be said for the appearance of the species. He often looks ragged and even in the best of condition would not command a second look. But for sheer volume of music there is no equal to the Gray Singing Finch. He is only four inches long, but makes up for his diminutive size with loud and constant melody. He more than justifies his place in a mixed collection.

The only way of sexing the Gray Singing Finch is to catch the male singing. Otherwise the sexes are indistinguishable. They will breed in a planted aviary and have been hybridized with domestic canaries.

Both Green and Gray Singing Finches are very easily cared for. They take a regular finch mixture but should also have more greenfood than most other finches.

Gray Singing Finch (male).

Cuban Finches

The Cuban Finches were more plentiful in North America prior to Fidel Castro than they are now, but a few are available from breeders in this country, and some are finding their way from Cuba to European dealers and then back to the United States. There are two species of Cuban finches of special interest for song.

The Cuban Melodious Finch (*Tiaris canora*) is a tiny, pudgy, vivacious bundle of energy about three inches long and very colorful. Most of his body is olive green, but he has a head that is very bright yellow with a black mask. He sings a busy warble as he flits incessantly about the flight. The female is similarly colored but unmistakably plainer.

The Melodious breeds best in a planted aviary, but does quite well in a cage. I remember seeing hundreds of them in bamboo cages about 6 inches cubed being sold in the markets and variety stores of Cuba when I lived there in 1957. They were selling for less than a dollar a pair, including the cage. We had a pair nesting in our front yard, and I was much impressed by the similarity in habits between our native wren and the Cuban Melodious. They put out a lot of sound for such a small body; they seem to have perpetual motion working for them, and they chatter a saucy song as they go about gathering a mountainous supply of live food for their voracious offspring.

I have always been a bit puzzled by writers who assert that the Melodious is misnamed. He has a delightful song that is frequently aired, and I consider him a distinctly musical bird. He makes an excellent addition to any mixed collection of small birds. He can become pugnacious when in breeding condition (a trait shared by most otherwise amicable birds), but he is not normally a troublemaker.

The other Cuban Finch to be mentioned is the Olive Finch (*Tiaris olivacea*), a near relative of the Melodious. The Olive is less colorful than the Melodious, although a bit larger. He is a general olive color with orange on the throat and an orange line running through the eye.

Both Cuban Finches thrive on small millet and small canary

seed, plus greenfood. I give mine the regular finch mixture and they pick out what they want of it, leaving the rest for species that have a slightly different appetite.

Shama Thrushes

The Shama Thrush (*Copsychus malabaricus indicus*) is certainly one of the most melodious of all birds. In addition to a glorious song, he offers a winning personality that makes him ideal as a cagebird. He is friendly, readily develops confidence in the members of his human family, and gets to the point where he can be given the liberty of the house and, in safe settings, of the garden as well.

The Shama is an attractive bird despite his very somber colors. His upper parts are black, his underparts chestnut, and his rump white. The snappy black eyes are large and prominent.

But the Shama's main claim to fame is his song, an unusually rich and clear melody with some of the warm quality of our Red-Winged Blackbird, some of the fullness of the American robin, and the liquid tones of a nightingale. For song, the Shama is unexcelled.

Both fortunately and unfortunately, the Shama is an accomplished mimic. If there are cardinals or other musical birds around, he is likely to make their notes a part of his own considerable repertoire. This is fortunate. But he never had a course in music appreciation, and he is just as likely to pick up the noise of a starling or a magpie—a good example of how environment enhances or corrupts!

Part of his attraction is the impertinent air with which he conducts himself. He switches his inordinately long tail about with an air of self-sufficiency that bespeaks disdain for everyone around him. He is fearless around human beings and around other feathered creatures; he exudes an air of confidence toward everyone he meets.

Although he does not give one the impression of being vicious, he must be kept away from other birds of the same or allied species. I learned this lesson indelibly a few years ago when I unexpectedly got a shipment of twelve Shamas and twelve Dhyals directly from India. I was to be gone for the evening, and in my haste I failed to see the significance of the fact that they were all in individual compartments. I divided them into several medium-sized flights, put food, bathing troughs, and electric lights in each flight and then left them for about twelve hours. When I got back the next morning, I had one vigorous bird left in each flight— the victor after a night of battle! That taught me not to mix Shamas with each other or with their closest relatives, the Dhyals. They will mix with some other species, however. And the transcendent beauty of the Shama song and his infectious personality make him more than worth the slight inconvenience of his pugnacity.

Both Dhyals and Shamas eat insectivorous food, live food, and fruit. Both love to bathe and will go through gallons of water if available.

Dhyal or Magpie Robin

Another Indian songster is the Dhyal Robin (*Copsychus saularis*), closely related to the Shama. Both are about the same size (10 inches long), but the Dhyal has more color. He is black above and white underneath, with some white in his wings and outer feathers of his tail. Another name is Magpie Robin, and he looks just as you would expect a bird with that name to look. The females are brown and gray.

The most expressive part of the Dhyal is his tail. He has skill in communicating his mood by a flick of the tail, expressing exasperation, anger, curiosity, challenge, and—but rarely—fear. He is an inquisitive creature, sizing up every part of his environment carefully.

Both the Shama and the Dhyal range rather widely throughout Southeast Asia but most of those imported to North America come from India. Rapid air service makes it possible for them to arrive the day after they leave India, but it is nevertheless a rugged experience, and buyers are wise to be sure the birds have been here long enough to adjust to their new home. Freight runs somewhat higher than usual because each Shama and Dhyal must be shipped in a separate compartment to avoid fighting and certain death for all but one.

Both species can be placed with birds not closely related, but they should be watched for a while. I would not trust them with birds smaller than weavers; the other birds should have plenty of room to get out of the way. Shamas and Dhyals do most of their singing very early in the morning and late at night, sometimes singing long after dark. Having one in an outdoor planted aviary will awaken the neighborhood daily to a cheerful mood.

Pekin Nightingale or Japanese Robin

Another bird with real musical charm is the Pekin Nightingale or Japanese Robin (*Leiothrix lutea*). His song is the richest and warmest full-throated warble of any of the commonly imported softbills. It has much of the quality with which an American robin greets the sun on an April morning after an all-night rain. As mentioned at the beginning of this chapter, one year I had a pair of Pekins in the flight that sits between our living room and bedroom, and I think not once while they were there did either my wife or I get up grouchy. Nor did we use the mechanical alarm clock. The

Pekin Nightingale (moulting around head).

Pekins must come from a long line of sun worshippers, because as soon as the first streak of dawn appeared, they began their serenades. What a lovely way to be awakened in the morning!

The Pekin is a lovely bird to see, as well as to hear. Although the basic color is olive, one is so impressed with the face and breast that he is inclined to describe the bird as yellow and orange. The wings have red, yellow, and orange feathers, also. The beak is peculiarly shaped; it is long and narrow and cherry red.

Pekins are about the fastest birds I know, short of hummingbirds. I have never seen a bird that could change position as fast as they.

Pintail Whydah (male in full color).

It is no exaggeration to say that you can be looking at a bird sitting eastbound on a twig, then suddenly realize that he has switched tail and head while you were looking at him and is now westbound. His speed of movement is fantastic. One year I had several in a flight, and they developed the habit of darting under my arm and through the feeding door when I opened it. Then it was a madhouse to try to catch them with a net in the birdroom. They seemed to know what move I was going to make even before I did. I finally had to vacate a large flight at the end of the room so I could leave its front open and chase them into it in order to get close to them.

The Pekin mixes well with other birds. I do not recall ever having one that gave any trouble to other birds. Feeding is simple. They consume a lot of fruit and mealworms, plus an insectivorous mixture. They live long and well on such a diet. They are about seven inches long.

There is no fool-proof way of sexing the Pekin Robin. Males sing and females twitter, which is half the solution, perhaps. Females tend to be less brightly colored than males, but an old female may outshine a young male.

The eight species discussed in this chapter certainly do not cover all the musical birds available in this country. There are several others that make enchanting music, but because of color or other characteristics, they are discussed in other chapters.

2

Brightly Colored Birds

ONE OF THE MAIN reasons why exotic cagebirds have gained in popularity so rapidly has been their great diversity of beautiful colors. Every conceivable color of the rainbow (and even some not in the rainbow) can be found on birds now commonly available in this country. Most of these birds will mix amicably with others of similar size, and you can make quite a glamorous collection by judicious selection of colors.

Several of the species described give the additional thrill of going from eclipse to nuptial plumage. This is one of the great wonders of nature and a thrill to watch. Within a few weeks a drab brown bird resembling our female English sparrow becomes a dazzling, steel-blue bird with white beak, the male Combassou in full breeding color. It is well worth the few months of drabness to watch the dramatic metamorphosis of these birds. They stay in color for several months, and then, just as suddenly, moult out of their glory and become plain again. This happens only to males; females do not assume breeding season "clothes."

"Painted Finch"

In the discussion of the Strawberry Finch in Chapter 1, I mentioned the "Painted Finch" that some Indian dealers create by dipping immature birds, females and males out of color, in vegetable dye. These are brilliantly colored birds, and I have seen them in bright shades of red, green, yellow, and lavender. Anyone buying such birds should be aware that the change may be only in one direction. After the lavender is moulted out in a few weeks, you may have a very un-lavender bird indefinitely.

Combassou (going into eclipse plumage).

But on the other hand, the bird under the surface may also be a very lovely fellow that will show exciting color and/or song later. The species most often dyed in this manner are Spicebirds, Silverbills, and Strawberry Finches.

Combassou

The Combassou (*Hypochera chalybeata*) was described at the opening of this chapter, but perhaps a little more information is appropriate. He is a rather small African species, about four inches long. In his glory he is a dazzling creature of glossy steel-blue, with white underwings, red legs, and white beak. When in color, he is invariably immaculate, not a feather being out of place. Females remain a plain brown-striped bird throughout the year. The male has nothing that could be termed a song. It is interesting to know that this gorgeous species is completely parasitic, not bothering to build a nest of its own. The hen notes where the nests of Firefinches are and when ready to lay pops into a nest momentarily

Baya Weaver.

untended, lays an egg, then moves on. Combassous are always peaceful. Technically this bird is a member of the Whydah family. He eats a standard finch seed mixture.

Weavers

There is a rather large group of colorful birds with an interesting pastime, the weavers. Several of these have brilliant nuptial plumage that they put on during our winter season in North America. But at any time in the year they may take a notion to weave a tapestry on the wires of the cage. They will use whatever is available—strips of newspaper, grass, cloth, or feathers—but if you will cooperate by furnishing short lengths of colored knitting yarn, they will create a masterpiece of impressionistic three-dimensional art. At Smithsonian's Zoo in Washington, D. C., they used to have a large flight filled with weavers, and with colored yarn the birds had festooned three branches with a frolic of pastel colors.

The most commonly imported of the weavers are the Orange Weaver (*Euplectes orix franciscana*) and the Napoleon Weaver (*Euplectes afra*). (See illustration, p. 103.) For our purposes it is sufficient to say that everything that applies to the Orange applies also to the Napoleon, except that the latter is a bright canary yellow where the other has orange or red. Both are about four inches long and come from Africa in large numbers. They are quarrelsome toward smaller birds than themselves, but get along with others of their own family or size. Sometimes weavers are called Bishops, presumably because their fluffy plumage resembles the traditional attire of some ecclesiastics. None of them have anything that could be termed a song, although they do make sounds of various kinds, mostly harsh ones.

It is curious that the name of the most common species is Orange Weaver, when the pictures show it to be red, not orange, in color. The reason for this is found in the fact that the red in the plumage of most species of birds in their natural state turns orange after the first moult in captivity. No one is certain what it is, but there is something missing from the artificial diet of captivity. Some patented products are now on the market to produce the color, but they are artificial and are not the missing natural element. In any case, the Orange Weaver is a rich orange when he has moulted in captivity, but newly caught specimens are a bright red.

The fiery orange or red feathers occur in an Elizabethan-ruff type of frilly cape that surrounds the neck and chest, setting off the velvety jet black head. Long plumes of the same orange or red shade arise at the rump and cascade over the brown tail, thus concealing it. The hen is an unimaginative combination of shades of brown.

There are other species of weavers that are imported, including the Red-Billed (*Quelea quelea*) and the Baya (*Ploceus philippinus*). (The Red-Billed is pictured on page 111.) I had an outdoor flight with two pairs of each of these two species last summer, and they built nests industriously all summer long. I do not think any hen laid, but they had a picnic starting housekeeping. As one pair would just about finish building a shapely bag about twelve inches long, suspended between the forks of a tree, another pair would sneak in when no one was looking and borrow some material. The birds tore weeds and grasses into long, thin strips up to a foot long for weaving purposes. And the last nests they built still look solid after several months of bad winter storms. The birds are not in them, of course. They are inside the house for the winter. All the weavers thrive on a balanced finch seed mixture.

Cordon Bleu

Also from Africa is a very pretty little waxbill, the Cordon Bleu (*Uraeginthus bengalus*). It is about four inches long. The brownish upper parts go unnoticed because all one can see is the bright sky-blue of the cheeks, neck, and breast. The male has a curious large crimson gash over each ear, so sexing is simple. Cordons breed well in a planted aviary.

The Cordon is a perfectly peaceful species. I have never seen one involved in a fight. They mix well with all small finches and other waxbills, sharing with the others the desire to squeeze as many birds onto a perch or into a nestbox as possible. There may

Cordon Bleu (hen).

be other totally unoccupied perches in the cage, but one high perch will end up so heavily populated that the birds are actually sitting two deep on each other's backs.

The Cordon Bleu thrives on a regular finch mixture and adjusts well to cage life.

Cutthroat Finch (Ribbon Finch)

Not a waxbill, but otherwise from Africa is the interesting Cutthroat Finch (*Amadina fasciata*), an attractive five-inch bird of brown tones. Each feather seems to be edged with a darker shade of brown, giving a lacy effect. Even the female is an attractive bird, but the male has an unmistakable feature, a bright red slit from ear to ear—really a bit gruesome if you make the connection. Perhaps the bird's other name is less offensive, Ribbon Finch.

The Cutthroat male has an interesting song and dance for his lady love. At the right moment he sticks out his feathers in all di-

Cutthroat Finches (male has red throat marking).

rections like a pincushion, stretches his neck as high as it will go, and then minces through a ludicrous song that always reminds me of a Mexican maraca, the musical gourd containing a few rasping pebbles.

Cutthroats breed readily in aviary or cage. They prefer a wooden nestbox about 5 inches cubed, in which they build a nest of twigs, grasses, yarn, paper, and feathers. I have seen them use a gourd or a wicker nest basket, also. They are sturdy birds, fairly peaceful, and are among the best for anyone who wants to start raising exotic cagebirds.

Lavendar Finch

Quite a different color is the Lavendar Finch (*Estrilda caerulescens*), another peaceful African waxbill. The color pattern is simple: a soft blue gray all over, except for a crimson rump and central tail feathers. The beak is red, and there is a black streak running from the beak through the eye. Tiny white specks are usually found on the flanks. Both sexes are alike. Length is about four inches.

Although they can get along on a seed diet, Lavendars seem to need live food a bit more than other waxbills. They will breed in planted aviaries but need considerable live food for feeding their babies. This need has been met successfully by some clever fanciers who have learned that opening the door of the flight when Lavendars have babies to feed enables them to find their own live food. Then when the babies leave the nest, they are placed in a large-mesh cage inside the flight to prevent their dispersal. The parents continue to feed the babies through the wires until weaned, at which time the door is closed during the night, and presto, the babies are raised, the parents are back home, and the fancier is proud of himself.

African Fire Finch

The African Fire Finch (*Laganosticta senegala*) is quite commonly imported. It is a small bird about three inches long. The female is mouse-colored and retiring. The male is a soft crimson all over, except for wings and tail, which tend more toward brown. The sizeable fleshy circle around the eye is an unusual feature among finches. Tiny white spots speckle the sides of the breast.

Fire Finches breed very easily in aviaries, and they can be given their liberty as described for Lavendar Finches. They are amicable, rarely engaging in any fight with other birds. They are extremely sociable, sitting as close to each other as the laws of physics allow— and sometimes appearing to break the law. Food is small finch millet or finch mixture.

Star Finch

Practically all of the specimens you see of the preceding birds in this chapter are wild-caught birds shipped to North America for sale. The next bird is quite a different case. The Star Finch is a native of Australia, but nearly all of the birds for sale in this country are cagebred, most of them in Japan.

A few years ago the Australian government placed a complete embargo on the exportation of any native birds except by permit and then only to legitimate public zoos. This was and is a controversial law, but it still stands. The result was disastrous to many trappers and businessmen who had become established in the trade. Australian hookbills and finches had dominated the exotic cage-bird fancy in America, and the supply was suddenly cut off.

Australia is a vast country, and there are thousands of square miles of land inhabited only by wild life, especially in the northern part. In these areas devoid of human habitation are countless birds of interest to fanciers around the world, and it seems improper to my prejudiced mind that Australia should ban their exportation. In some farming areas, flocks of cockatoos descend like a tragedy, wiping out a farmer's work overnight. Yet the farmer is not permitted to capture the voracious things and sell them to recoup part of his loss.

This law has created two by-products. First, smuggling of Australian birds has increased. When I was in Singapore in 1964 there were dealers openly trafficking in Australian birds smuggled out by sailors. Some of the rarest of Australian birds were on the shelves and one dealer told me he has a standing order to ship as many of certain species as he can get to a Dutch importer-exporter, regardless of price. Since smuggled birds are usually not in the care of people who know birds and love them, they tend to be handled in unsanitary conditions that breed disease and weaken the stock.

The second by-product of the ban is a happy one. In view of the impending shortage of Australian birds there was a strong impetus to breed them in captivity. The result has been many, many more cage- and aviary-bred specimens of Australian birds. The Japanese have been especially successful at this. Because of their great love for nature and the limitations of their living space, Japanese aviculturists have worked diligently at cage-breeding species previously available only as wild-trapped birds. They have domesticated such finches as Shaft-Tails, Parsons, Parrot Finches, and Lady Goulds (see Chapter 4). All of these come from Japan now in considerable numbers, especially the Lady Gould. But another species is becoming almost as commonly available, the Star Finch.

The Star Finch (*Bathilda ruficauda*) is sometimes referred to as the Ruficauda. It is a delightfully colored bird about five inches long. Most of the body is chartreuse. The face, forehead, and throat

African Fire Finch (male).

are vermilion, with countless tiny white spots. Stars always impress me as appearing perpetually embarrassed, since they blush constantly. The female is similarly marked, but does not blush quite so brightly.

The male has an interesting courting dance. He likes to get the longest stalk of grass within reach and hold it by one end in his beak, waving it to and fro. Sometimes it overbalances him and he tumbles off the perch, but since his face was red already he is able to resume the stance without looking perturbed in the least. Breeding habits are similar to those of the Lady Gould, described in Chapter 4.

Stars do very well on a standard finch seed mixture and greenfood. When they are breeding, they need spray millet, flowering grasses, and live food, as well. They are very peaceful birds and can be mixed safely with smaller species.

Buntings

This is an entire family of birds that should be discussed together. A few of each species are on the market, and it is difficult

Poker-Headed Weaver (male).

to narrow the list down to just one or two. The following two are the most common.

The Indian Yellow or Red-Headed Bunting (*Emberiza bruniceps*) is an attractive-looking bird that is quiet and friendly with other birds and has a pleasant call. He is about seven inches long, has brown upper parts and bright yellow underparts. How he got the name of "Red-Headed" I do not know; he has an outstanding head and throat of rich·chestnut, but there is not a red feather on his body. The female is very plain.

Although his attractive coloration would lead you to think the Red-Headed would be a popular species, he is not. He is relatively inactive and has as nearly no personality as any bird I know. He is, as a schoolteacher would say, "a good middle 'C'."

From Mexico comes the Rainbow Bunting (*Passerina leclancheri*), perhaps the most colorful of the buntings. The upper parts are turquoise, the neck cobalt, the forehead green, the breast orange, and the underparts yellow. Females are colored similarly but are so much more subdued in brilliance that sexing adult birds is simple. More than other birds already discussed in this chapter, the Rainbow needs live food. He should have insectivorous mixture and some mealworms or other live food in addition to the regular finch seed mixture.

Tanagers

A family even more difficult to summarize than the buntings is the tanager family. Importers often refuse even to give names for species they have since there are so many, and identification calls for an expert ornithologist with a large reference library. But most of the tanagers are gorgeous creatures of brilliant hue that are a delight to own.

In general, tanagers should be offered a good insectivorous food mixture, plus various kinds of fruit and live food. Bread moistened with milk, sometimes laced with honey, is relished. Soaked raisins and chopped dates may also be welcomed. Soya flour may aid in maintaining the red color during the moult.

Perhaps the most common tanager available in this country is the Scarlet (*Rhamphocelus brasilius*) from Brazil, as distinguished from the species of the same name native to North America (*Piranga olivacea*). It is about seven inches long, has a scarlet body and velvety black back, wings, and tail. The female is reddish-brown.

The Paradise Tanager (*Tangara paradisea*) is small (five inches) and comes from the Guianas. Its upper parts are a vivid sky blue, except for the black shoulders, wings, and tail, which set off and make the blue even more dramatic. The head is an iridescent golden green. All of this is dazzling when seen in the sunlight against green foliage.

Bulbuls

Another group of birds now becoming available to North American fanciers in increasing numbers is the Indian Bulbul family, and two species in particular.

The Red-Whiskered Bulbul (*Pycnonotus jocosus*) is an especially alert bird. His permanently erect crest curves forward in a quizzical manner, like a huge black question-mark. His lines are cardinal-like, as are his determined, sure mannerisms. He is basically gray and white elsewhere. In addition to the very impressive crest, he has a debonair red whisker on each cheek and a bright red vent. Red-Whiskered Bulbuls readily become tame, and although fairly large (seven inches), they are not a threat to smaller species. They have a *bon vivant* air about them that makes them a favorite in either cage or aviary, and they have a pleasant song.

So attractive is the Red-Whiskered that for years I have used one on my letterhead as a symbol of what personality and beauty an exotic cagebird can present.

The other commonly imported bulbul is the Red-Vented (*Pycnonotus cafer*). This bird is a somber slate color, lightening toward the underparts. He is about seven inches long, and he has a bulky crest which he can raise or lower at will. His distinguishing feature, as the name indicates, is the bright red spot around the vent. (See illustration, p. 110.)

Bulbuls are highly frugivorous, consuming bananas, oranges, apples, and especially grapes by the sackful. I have found them usually fond of bread moistened with milk, laced with honey, too. Because of their diet, the paper in their cage must be changed more frequently than for seedeaters, but this is no serious problem for anyone who really cares for them.

Cardinals

Similar to the size, shape, and personality of the bulbuls but different in diet and song is the group of cardinals on the market in North America. The gorgeous red Virginia Cardinal (*Richmondena cardinalis*) that is native to much of the United States cannot be kept legally, of course.

Red-Whiskered Bulbul.

There is, however, a Brazilian species that is very similar but different enough that it can be kept legally. It is the Venezuelan Red Cardinal (*Cardinalis cardinalis*). This bird lacks some of the glaring brilliance of its North American counterpart, but it is nevertheless a beautiful bird. It is red all over except for a black bib. The bird is really a grosbeak and shares that family's stately manner. He has a penetrating song which can be heard throughout the neighborhood. In addition to a budgie seed mixture, he should have hemp and sunflower, plus apple and greenfood. A few mealworms now and then will be appreciated. Red Cardinals become tame readily, especially when enticed with morsels like mealworms.

Three other kinds of cardinals are also imported. These are not closely related to the foregoing, however; they are nearer to buntings than to grosbeaks. Two of these are almost identical except that one lacks a crest: the Pope Cardinal (*Paroaria dominicana*) and the Red-Crested Cardinal (*Paroaria cucullata*). They are about seven inches long (the Pope perhaps a shade smaller), and come from western South America. Upper parts are gray and underparts white. The head and throat are bright red, and in the Red-Crested, the tall crest is also a brilliant scarlet.

Red-Crested Cardinal.

The other popular cardinal is the Green Cardinal (*Gubernatrix cristata*). The male is green above, yellow underneath, with darker markings on the tail and wings. There is a black goatee, and the crest is black. Usually the crest is carried at rest, but it can be raised at will. The adult Green is about seven inches long. Females are noticeably more quietly attired than males, so sexing is easy. This species is native to Argentina. The Green Cardinal breeds fairly well in planted aviaries. (See illustration, p. 107.)

Saffron Finch

Another colorful South American bird is the Saffron Finch (*Sicalis flaveola*). It is about six inches long, is greenish yellow on the upper parts, merging to yellow on the underparts. The head is orange, the forehead and crown being a bright orange, giving him his name of Saffron. Females are similar but more dull.

The Saffron may on occasion become a bully, so if mixed with smaller species, it should be watched, especially when breeding season approaches. They thrive on a regular finch seed mixture, plus greenfood and an occasional mealworm. Some will take a soft-bill mixture, also. The Saffron can be acclimatized to spend a northern winter outside.

Golden Song Sparrow

A bird rather similar to the Saffron but from northeastern Africa instead of South America is the Golden Song Sparrow (*Auripasser luteus*). About the same size as the Saffron, the Golden is a bright yellow with brownish wings and tail and a black beak. The female is more brown than yellow. These birds are sometimes sold as Golden Sparrows or as Yellow Sparrows. They mix well with the larger finches but may be a threat to smaller ones. This species and the Saffron are ideal answers for people who are looking for exotic birds to share a flight with budgies.

Waxbills

For energy per ounce there is nothing on the market to match the tiny waxbill family. It is a large family, the best known member of which is from India, the Strawberry Finch. The Cordon Bleu is another popular waxbill. Both of these species are discussed elsewhere in this book. Since their names do not indicate the fact, most people do not think of them as waxbills.

But there are three perfectly delightful African birds clearly labeled as waxbills that would be welcome in any home. They are the Gray, the Orange-Cheeked, and the Golden-Breasted.

The Gray Waxbill (*Estrilda troglodytes*), also called Common, Red-Eared, and Red-Rumped Waxbill, is perpetual motion itself. It is a soft tan-gray all over except for a rosy red vent and a red streak that runs from the beak through the eye. The beak is bright red and the legs black. Length is under four inches, but the bird is so active it is difficult to catch it still long enough to gauge size. Particularly entrancing is its habit of twitching its tail in a perky manner as it lands on perch or wire.

The Orange-Cheeked Waxbill (*Estrilda melpoda*) is a little larger than the preceding and is more colorful. In addition to the general delicate fawnish coloring, this species has large bright orange cheeks that give it distinction among the waxbills.

The Golden-Breasted Waxbill (*Estrilda s. subflava*) is the tiniest of all commonly imported birds; it is so small that some stores do not like to carry it because it can escape from most cages. There are several races and the colors vary somewhat, but all of them are very pretty. The male is brownish-green in the upper parts, with a bright orange breast that merges to red in the center and toward the belly. The sides have vertical stripes of gray. Altogether the little fellow is barely more than three inches long.

All three of these species are remarkably simple to care for. They are completely peaceful with all other birds and will never start a fight. They are highly resistant to common illnesses, they thrive in cages, and remain wonderfully cheerful under ordinary circumstances.

Food is no problem. These waxbills get along well on either small millet or a finch mixture. Most individuals will not touch fruit, but if they will take it or greens, it is a good idea to make the offer occasionally.

Golden-Breasted Waxbill (foreground) and Common or Red-Eared Waxbill.

These waxbills will gladly build a nest in a wicker globe or in a box 5 inches cubed, with half the front open. They use fine grasses, twine, paper, and feathers. All the waxbills you have in the cage will pile into the same box without scrapping. I have counted as many as ten little red beaks pointing at me out of the same nest. If conditions are right, some of them will stake out a claim to a nest, lay, and raise young ones on the same diet, although while they are feeding babies it is a good idea to offer them live food.

Saffron Finch.   *Golden Song Sparrow (male).*

Orange-Cheeked Waxbill (note overgrown beak and nails).

Mannikins

There is a family of southeastern Asian birds called mannikins or nuns that supplies a major proportion of the exotic cagebirds commonly available in this country. They are birds of attractive but somber coloration, perfectly peaceful around other birds, and readily adaptable to domesticated surroundings. The first two of the following are quite common, and the third is fairly so.

The Black-Headed Nun (*Munia atricapilla*) is a rich chocolate color all over, except for jet black that covers the head, upper breast, and underside of the tail. He is about four inches long.

The Tri-Colored Nun (*Munia malacca*) is a shade larger and is colored the same shades of warm brown and black but with a slightly different pattern. The upper parts are brown, the head and upper breast black, the lower chest and abdomen white, and the vent area black. (See illustration, p. 114.)

The third species of mannikins differs from the preceding two in that it is African in origin and is smaller, about three inches long. At first glance the Bronze-Winged Mannikin (*Spermestes cucullatus*) appears to be a simple black and white bird, but in the proper angle with the source of light there is a striking bronze sheen on the wings. Although the Black-Headed and the Tri-Colored look enough alike to be color varieties of the same species, the Bronze-

Winged is quite different in body formation, bearing, and coloration. The former two are much less active and sit more upright than the latter, and perhaps the fact that they are less nervous is one of the reasons why they are more popular with bird dealers. Their needs are simple, and they withstand crowded conditions better, also.

Even wild-trapped specimens of these three species may breed in cage or aviary. They seem to take best to wicker baskets, gourds, or 5-inch-cubed boxes with the front half open. They will use anything they can find for nesting material but especially welcome fine dry grasses, short pieces of yarn, and feathers.

The Tri-Colored and the Black-Headed both have problems with overgrown nails in cage life. For simple instructions on how to control this see Chapter 6.

Mannikins should not be confused with Manakins, a group of very brightly colored birds from Central and South America. The latter are frugivorous and insectivorous, seldom imported and never available except through dealers in very rare birds.

Spicebird

Closely related to the Tri-Colored and Black-Headed Nuns is the Spicebird (*Munia punctulata*), sometimes also called Nutmeg Finch. This bird has the characteristic rich brown over most of the body, but the breast and upper abdomen are covered with white feathers delicately edged with a fine brown line, producing a lovely lacy, all-over scalloped effect. This color pattern is unique to the Spicebird and may even be recognized through the lurid shades of dye some Indian dealers use to brighten up the appearance of their birds.

The Striated Finch (*Munia striata*) is quite similar except that his breast feathers are brown with whitish edging. Both of these birds are about four inches long and come from India. Their needs are the same as those of the Black-Headed and Tri-Colored Nuns.

Silverbills

The Silverbill could almost as well be discussed in the chapter on "The Well Domesticated" as here, except that the rule for that chapter is that all specimens on the market must have been raised in cage or aviary. The Silverbill breeds with great freedom in confinement, but most of the birds available to the American public were trapped, so they are discussed in this chapter.

Actually there are two kinds of Silverbills on our market, depending on their place of origin. To the casual observer they will look alike, but when seen side by side one can readily note a difference. The darker ones come from India (*Euodice malabarica*) and the lighter from Africa (*Euodice cantans*). They interbreed without the slightest hesitation, and among cagebred specimens the distinction is soon lost.

The Silverbill is about four inches long and has a pleasant combination of brown and white, the white being on the breast. In a bird in good condition the tail comes to a point. The name comes from the blue-gray sheen the bill takes on when the bird is in breeding condition. I have always thought "silver" was a bit of an overstatement, but sometimes overstatements have a way of creeping into birds' names. The sexes look alike but if one keeps a few Silverbills in a cage, before long each of the males will be seen in a grotesque posture, prancing up and down on the perch, singing his soft but quite musical sound.

Silverbills are completely amiable birds and almost never cause trouble in a flight, unless it would be to "borrow" nesting material from another nest. They are easy birds to raise and general instructions are the same as those for Zebra Finches in Chapter 4.

A simple diet of large and small millet or finch mixture will keep Silverbills in good condition. They are such reliable birds and so easily cared for that many Japanese aviculturists use them as foster parents to raise the young of more difficult species. Silverbills are excellent birds for the beginner in breeding exotic cagebirds.

Java Sparrow

Names can be unfortunate labels at times and the Java Sparrow (*Padda oryzivora*) is one of the victims. He is really a very attractive bird with many highly desirable qualities, and it is too bad that

Two shots of the popular Bronze-Winged Mannikin.

the overtones we associate with the word "sparrow" should be laid to his account. This has been circumvented by one major importer who has had large posters printed on which the Java's name was

African Silverbill (left) and Spicebird.

changed to "Sacred Temple Bird." This is not accurate, but it is an improvement, and I am sure many more have homes as Sacred Temple Birds than would have made it had they been labeled sparrows.

It is almost impossible to find a Java that is in less than immaculate appearance. He is always spotless, perfectly groomed. His basic color is a medium gray, with black cap, white breast, mauve abdomen, large white cheek spots, and black tail. The most prominent feature is an immense, bright red beak. It is a thick, deep-set beak that somehow manages to miss looking grotesque despite its oversize. About five inches long, the Java is a handsome bird, indeed.

The sexes look alike. The only way to determine a male is to hear him singing, and a female only by having her lay an egg. It is said that a male in breeding condition has a brighter beak swollen a bit at the base, but this is a difficult factor to gauge. Two bachelors or two spinsters will cooperate in building a nest and the spinsters will take turns incubating the blank eggs, so having them build a nest is no guarantee. Do not take orders for the babies unless one of the two sings and the other lays eggs.

The song of the male is rich and mellow, and as he sings he dances a bit to bewitch his beloved. He hunches his shoulders forward, ducks his head, and glances over his glasses at his paramour, all the time prancing rhythmically up and down on the perch. Javas use a nestbox about 6 inches cubed. I have found a budgie nestbox to

Gray Java Sparrow.

Red-Headed Bunting (male).

be quite satisfactory, although the Java does not need a concave bottom. He builds a well-organized nest of grasses and twigs. If you are looking for a finch that will mix well with budgies, the Java is a good choice. His color is contrasting, he is able to defend himself against a cantankerous old "grandmother," and he does well on the budgie diet. Javas are not too safe to put with smaller birds in a small cage where a bully can persecute a victim, but they do well with other birds their size or larger. And in larger enclosures they ordinarily do not cause any problem with smaller birds.

The preceding description applies to the inexpensive color variety ordinarily on the market, the Normal Gray Java Sparrow. There is another color occasionally for sale, the White. And a gorgeous bird it is. All Whites are bred in confinement; they do not occur in the wild. There are only three colors on the bird: the huge red beak, snappy black eyes, both set in a dazzling snow-white bird—beautiful! The Calico Java Sparrow, a mottled variety, is rarely available.

Yellow-Winged Sugarbird

Occasionally you can find this gorgeous creature for sale, and it is hard to pass up the opportunity to acquire him. Nor is there good reason. The Yellow-Winged Sugarbird (*Cyanerpes cyaneus*) is a bird of supreme beauty, is quite a novelty, and although a nectarine is fairly easily cared for. (See illustration, page 102.)

The male in breeding plumage is a noble sight. He has shiny jet black tail, wings, and neck. Most of the rest of the body is a striking royal blue. The crown and forehead are turquoise, almost iridescent in the right light. His legs are red and his long, slightly curved beak is black. His name comes from the canary-yellow underside of his wings, which shows only when he flies, but since he is an avid aerial acrobat this is frequently. Few birds of his size (about five inches) pack so much brilliant color into so small a package.

Yellow-Winged Sugarbirds come from northern South America. When out of breeding color the male resembles the hen, who is mostly green with a few brown stripes on her underparts. His change from eclipse plumage comes dramatically in a period of just a couple of weeks, and it is well worth buying him in his plain garb (if you can be certain it is a male) in order to watch the amazing change, like Cinderella before the ball.

All nectarine birds require daily attention to keep fresh nectar before them. The formulas are given in Chapter 6. In addition, the Yellow-Winged Sugarbird ought to have fruit to fit his particular appetite. Their tastes differ, but ripe banana, sweet orange, and grape are frequently preferred. I also offer fruit flies as much to see the bird's antics as to provide protein. It is amusing to watch him dart erratically around the cage in an effort to out-maneuver a fly so tiny as to be invisible to any bystander. A handy way to feed fruit flies is to expose overripe fruit to the air for a day, then place it in a plastic cup that has a hole the size of pencil lead in the cover. The Sugarbird will soon learn to sit near the cup and when a fly comes out of the hole an aerial duel worthy of Eddie Rickenbacker follows.

3

Hookbills and Talking Mynahs

ARCHEOLOGISTS HAVE DISCOVERED drawings that show pet parrots going back thousands of years. There is something particularly appealing about a bird that can imitate the human voice, and when the bird adds loyalty and longevity to his characteristics, he becomes a permanent fixture.

There are many hookbills on the market in the United States despite a tight ban on their importation since the early 1930's. Under federal law there were only two ways for parrot-family birds to come into the States. Licensed zoos could import them, but could not thereafter transfer them to anyone but another zoo. Or a private individual who had lived abroad and had had a parrot as a pet for a period of several months could bring the bird back, but must certify that he was not doing so for commercial purposes, and there was a strict limit as to how many and how often he could do this.

There was a reason for this "feather curtain" around the country. A contagious fever infecting human beings was discovered years ago, and it was traced to parrots in the homes of the victims. It was given the medical name of psittacosis (after *Psittacidae,* scientific

Salle's Parrot.

name of the parrot family) and the common name of Parrot Fever. It was determined correctly that the disease was carried by parrots kept in unsanitary conditions, especially by those being imported in large numbers and in small cages. In 1930 thirty deaths in the United States were attributed to the disease, so the almost absolute embargo was passed. On the basis of the knowledge then available it was good legislation.

But present knowledge makes the law obsolete. The disease is now being called not psittacosis, after parrots, but ornithosis, after birds. The most recent serious outbreak I have heard about was in a turkey-processing plant in Texas in 1963. Other sources of the fever have been traced to pigeons in city halls, ducks, chickens, pheasants, and wild waterfowl, in that order. I asked the head of a state department of health about the incidence of psittacosis or ornithosis in his state, and he did not know what the disease was. After I described it, he said he had heard about it in medical school but had never known of a case.

Modern antibiotics have rendered ornithosis almost harmless.

When detected, it responds readily to treatment and is no longer a serious threat to health. A few years ago an antibiotic treatment for entire flocks of birds was developed, either by injections into the birds or by mixing a substance with the feed. So although the disease was a genuine threat to human beings at the time the restrictive legislation was passed, it is no longer. The laws should be repealed, and at the time this book is being written the Public Health Service of the United States Department of Health, Education and Welfare is deeply engaged in final stages of a research project that is expected to pave the way for liberalizing the regulations governing the importation of parrot-family birds.

A number of large parrot-type birds are being kept in a South American country under a veterinarian's care, and they are being treated with chlorotetracycline to eradicate the psittacosis germs from their system. They will then be kept in several pet shops in this country for four months under conditions identical to those they would face if imported for commercial purposes. If the birds pass this final test, it will prove that birds thus treated medically can be safely placed on the open market, and once again it will become possible to import psittacine birds into the United States. They probably will have to be placed in government-inspected quarantine for a few weeks of treatment with chlorotetracycline and medical observation, but they will thereafter become available. The United States Public Health Service is to be greatly commended for diligent detective work in finding a solution to this threat to the health of us all. First, they eliminated the threat of death to human beings afflicted with the disease. No death has been reported in the United States since 1958. And now they have succeeded in finding an agent that will eliminate the disease completely even from the birds themselves. And this means the laws can be changed to meet the new conditions.

In the meantime, parrot-family birds in the United States are inordinately expensive. I recall the first macaw I priced in Mexico years ago. The asking price—usually at least double the expected price—was $15.00 for a lovely tame Scarlet Macaw. In Illinois it would have sold for $300.00.

The scarcity of psittacine birds has produced artificially high prices, and this has attracted unethical people. The border patrol a couple of years ago apprehended a man who had drugged a load of parrots and placed them in the gas tank of his car to avoid detection, having installed a second, temporary gas tank to get across the border. The last time I was in Nuevo Laredo I saw a man with about fifteen fledgling Mexican Double Yellow-Head Parrots clambering on top of a cage and playing with each other like a litter of puppies. We talked for a while and he told me he sold all he could get, usually making the deal for about $5.00 each. I am sure they would have brought $100.00 each in Chicago. "But," I said to get his reaction, "isn't it impossible to take them across the border?"

"Not in the least," he replied with a gesture toward his shirt front. "You just roll him in a handkerchief, place him inside your shirt, and walk across the bridge."

I am sure this is the way many of the parrots come into the United States. But most of the birds on the market are not contraband. Many species are now being bred in California (even the desirable African Gray), and people who have lived abroad bring their birds back and sell them subsequently. And since the life expectancy of most parrots is longer than their master's, there comes a time when someone else acquires each of them.

What parrot makes the best talker? It depends so much on the individual bird, but there seems to be agreement among the most experienced people that the two most likely species are the African Gray and the Mexican Double Yellow-Head.

African Gray Parrot

The African Gray Parrot (*Psittacus e. erithacus*) is a rather unorthodox parrot. In the first place, he does not have a green feather to his name. He is a soft gray all over, except for a bright red tail. There are shades of gray on different parts of the body, and the breast feathers are tipped with white, producing a "lacewing" effect.

The second unexpected feature of the Gray is his rather long

Half-Moon Parrot (note new head feathers coming out of sheaths).

and pointed head. Some call it snake-like, but I think this overdoes it. A large portion of the face is devoid of feathers, being a powdery white. Bill and feet are black. An adult bird has straw-colored eyes and is about thirteen inches long. Young birds have dark gray eyes.

As a family pet, the Gray has an added feature. More than any other species, he is able to reproduce fine tones of difference in people's voices, and his ability to speak realistically is so remarkable that he can create a minor crisis in a family by making an inappropriate remark at a most awkward moment, laying the blame on

Double Yellow-Head Parrot.

the person he is imitating. And a Gray with a sense of humor can drive the family dog frantic by whistling for him and calling, "Here, Rover; here, Rover."

Amazon Parrots

The Amazon Parrots constitute a genus of about fifty species, among which are found most of the pet parrots of the United States. All of the Amazons are native to the Americas. Most of them make good pets and most of them will learn to talk. They vary from quite small to quite large, and most of them are predominantly green.

When I lived in Puerto Rico some years ago I was just a few

miles from the Rain Forest on El Yunque, which is under the United States Park Service, and the wild parrots are, therefore, the only flock of indigenous parrots under their protection. It was a thrill to hear their cries come up the valley and to see their peculiar silhouettes against the sky: wide wings, stocky body, and tail, but apparently no head.

SALLE'S PARROT

Many Puerto Rican homes have pet Salle's Parrots (*Amazona ventralis*), delightful Amazons from nearby islands. The Salle's green feathers are edged with brownish pencilings that give a lacy effect on the breast and wings. There is a patch of white on the forehead. The most unusual feature is a large slate-gray patch over each ear. On the lower parts there are varying amounts of bright red feathers, in some cases as much as to produce red britches around the thighs. An occasional specimen will have a curious patch of red on the chin, like a tiny goatee. Salle's Parrots are rarely brought to the mainland of the United States, but a few do come, and the same is true of each of the other scarce species of Amazons. However, all Amazons combined form a sizeable quantity.

MEXICAN DOUBLE YELLOW-HEAD

There is some difference of opinion as to whether the African Gray should rule as king of the talking parrots. There are partisans who insist that the Mexican Double Yellow-Head Parrot (*Amazona ochrocephala oratrix*), also named Levaillant's Amazon Parrot, is the best talking parrot. I think both species show remarkable ability to reproduce the human voice, and individual specimens become fantastic mimics.

The Mexican Double Yellow-Head is much more common in this country than the Gray because his native land is much closer than Africa. He has a usually placid personality and, except for individuals who have been taught bad habits by human associates, makes a splendid pet. In addition to his talking ability, he has a facility for affection and quickly becomes a member of the family.

Only a small portion of the young bird's head is yellow, but as he grows older, the amount of yellow increases. There is also red on the wings and at the base of the tail, and blue on the wings. He is about 15 inches long.

YELLOW-NAPED AND PANAMA PARROTS

Another commonly seen species is closely related to the foregoing, the Yellow-Naped Amazon (*Amazona ochrocephala auropalliata*). This bird is usually a bit larger than the Double Yellow-Head, but otherwise it is very similar. It has the dark green characteristic of the Amazons but with a slight bluish sheen. The distinguishing characteristic is a patch of yellow on the back of the neck. There is also a small patch of yellow on the forehead (absent in the very young birds) and red, blue, and yellow portions in the wings and tail. The Yellow-Naped is reputedly a consistently excellent talker.

The importance of scientific bird names is illustrated by the confusion that exists in this country between the Yellow-Naped and the Panama Amazon Parrot (*Amazona ochrocephala panamensis*). The former is often sold as a "Panama Parrot." They are both green and both have the yellow forehead, but the true Panama is somewhat smaller and lacks the yellow patch on the back of the neck. The Panama comes from northern South America and the Panama Isthmus, while the Yellow-Naped ranges in southern Mexico. The first of the wild Yellow-Naped I saw was in the Tehuantepec Peninsula near the Mexico-Guatemala border one morning when a flock of several hundred of them landed in the tree over our house trailer. We had stopped alongside the road for the night and when dawn came, so did the birds. What a racket they made! But it was a thrilling one to me. A couple of days later I was stranded with car trouble in a small town nearby, and the mechanic had a gorgeous adult Yellow-Naped sitting in the patio. He was in full plumage and could have flown away but made no effort to do so. He was obviously a town pet; everyone who came near would speak to him cordially, and a few offered him tidbits.

MEXICAN RED-HEAD PARROT

One other Amazon is popular enough to warrant specific mention, the Mexican Red-Head (*Amazona viridigenalis*), more prop-

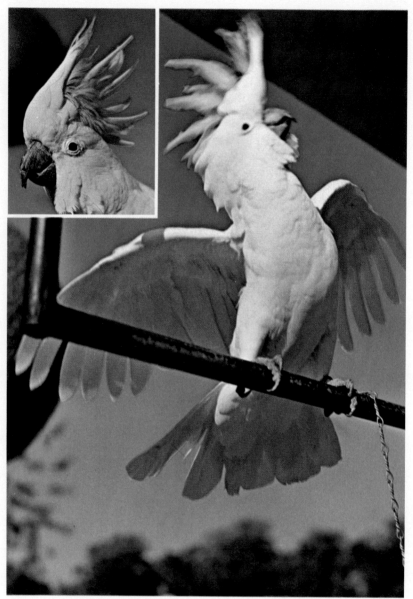

Sulphur-Crested Cockatoo displaying at Indianapolis Zoo.

Blue-and-Gold Macaw.

erly known as the Green-Cheeked Amazon Parrot. He is much smaller than the Double Yellow-Head but makes an excellent pet. Many individuals become good talkers, and most of them develop affectionate, trusting personalities.

The Red-Head is readily recognized. Young birds have less red showing, but older adults have large red caps that come down to the eyes. Some have a touch of lavender along the lower edge of the red. And the cheeks are bright green. Wings have red and blue. The beak is yellowish but no other yellow is found on the head.

There are many other Amazon Parrots that are available in the

United States, but the ones discussed here are the more common ones. All of them are potentially excellent pets, but it is wise to be sure you are not buying one whose personality has been marred by a human family that did not love him. Even a fierce bird can sometimes be reclaimed, but it does take many months of tender, loving care. Whenever I see a mean parrot I remind myself that he is spiteful because somewhere there is a mean human being who made him that way.

The Amazon Parrots and the African Gray eat a basic diet of sunflower, to which are added several other seeds, like hemp, oats groats, canary, and large white proso millet. The parrot mix distributed by a reputable seed dealer usually is quite adequate. Often it includes treats like hot pepper and peanuts too. The parrot should also receive fruit and greenfood, grit, and fresh water daily.

Sulphur-Crested Cockatoos

One of the most dramatic members of the hookbills is the Greater Sulphur-Crested Cockatoo (*Kakatoe galerita*). His coloring is extremely simple: black, white, and yellow. But the way in which these colors are arranged and displayed makes them most effective.

Set in the snowy white background, his snappy black eyes and his black feet and beak stand out. The huge crest is bright yellow, and when he raises it to express curiosity, anger, pleasure, or any other emotion, he steals the scene from any competitor. The Greater Sulphur-Crested is a large bird to start with, and his dazzling white body looks even larger. There are no colored feathers on his body other than the crest.

In their native Australian habitat these birds are a nuisance and farmers spend thousands of dollars a year to kill them. Australian farmers hunt, trap, and poison them much as American farmers fight crows. But the Australian government's ban on exportation and the U. S. government's ban on importation maintain an unnecessary scarcity of these birds in this country. In 1957, before the Australian ban was imposed, I saw perfectly tame Greater Sulphur-

Crested Cockatoos in Cuba for under $25.00 each, while ninety miles north in Florida they were bringing $400.00.

But one must be extremely cautious in purchasing one of these birds because of their fantastic powers of destruction. Their powerful beaks are fully capable of severing a human finger at one bite, and one that has developed distrust of man ought not to be offered very many experimental fingers.

I suppose no one in the country has more magical touch than Mrs. E. L. Moon, but I recall the way in which she entered the breeding flight of a pair of Greater Sulphur-Crested Cockatoos at Parrot Jungle, in Miami. She maneuvered in such a way that her eyes never left the pair, explaining that like a white tornado one could strike her viciously and leave her minus a few pounds of flesh.

If Mrs. Moon's birds merited caution, then people with less experience and know-how ought to be even more cautious. But I emphasize that this caution applies to strange birds. Many individuals of the same species are as gentle as kittens, and Mrs. Moon used to take a pet Greater Sulphur-Crested with her to Sunday School for the children to enjoy.

There is a similar species of Cockatoo sometimes available, the Lesser Sulphur-Crested (*Kakatoe sulphures*). Whereas the Greater is about twenty inches long, the Lesser is about twelve. The Lesser has a yellow cheek patch, but otherwise everything said about one species applies to the other. The Lesser comes from the island of Celebes rather than Australia.

For food the Sulphur-Cresteds take a good grade of sunflower, plus some canary, oats groats, hemp, and greens. They also appreciate bread moistened with milk, and fruit.

Macaws

The most colorful of the hookbills are the macaws, the large birds favored by artists and advertisers. And with reason—a good macaw is a gorgeous sight.

Although there are several other species kept as pets, two are by

Scarlet and Blue-and-Gold Macaws at Indianapolis Zoo.

far the most common, the Scarlet Macaw (*Ara macao*) and the Blue and Gold Macaw (*Ara ararauna*). The latter is sometimes called the Blue and Yellow Macaw, also, and I think it is probably more accurately descriptive. Both are handsome birds about thirty-six inches long and brightly colored.

The Scarlet, sometimes called the Red and Yellow Macaw, is a brilliant scarlet on the head, shoulders, and underparts, with bright blue flight feathers, yellow and green secondaries, and red and blue tail. His face is devoid of feathers, appearing a powdery white. Older birds are more brilliantly colored, but even young ones are very colorful.

I have a young Scarlet with which I am baby sitting at the moment. He has the freedom of the owner's backyard there and has come to feel that he owns everything he sees. His wings were clipped by the natives who got him from the nest, and he has not yet moulted back his wing feathers, but when he moved from tropical Costa Rica to Indiana he was plunged into a radical moult and his neck looks like a porcupine where the new feathers' sheaths are visible in large numbers. He speaks his name very clearly in Spanish, "Lapa," and I presume a little work by his master will make him bilingual at his new home. Because there was no one at home all day to keep him company I brought him to my office, where he gets to see people all day long. It is amusing to note how casually he takes a male visitor, but if a female walks in, he gets excited, moves about his cage erratically, and if she is wearing a coat, he may scream. I do not know what happened, but somewhere in his background I am sure he was mistreated by a woman, and he still has that fear of them. Or is he just a Don Juan?

I give him the freedom of the office for about fifteen minutes a day, and he climbs up and down chairs, the desk, and bookcases. But his favorite stance is a peculiar one; he loves to sit on the toe of my shoe. When I become engrossed in what I am doing and forget that he is about, suddenly I am snapped back with the realization that Lapa is contentedly perched on my toe. I give him a "horsie" ride a few times as I used to do to entertain my small children, then he contentedly climbs down and continues his inspection of the premises. But shortly he is back again and if I do not teeter him soon enough, he will pull my sock or pants cuff with his hooked beak. He is as personable as a puppy. One day he had climbed onto my shoulder when the janitor came in to get the wastepaper basket. I was reading, deep in thought, and Lapa had his head laid alongside my neck like a baby being burped. The janitor never has forgotten the scene.

The Blue and Gold Macaw is similar in size and personality. Its colors are quite different, however. The upper parts are a bright blue and the underparts are a bright yellow. The crown may have a greenish tinge, and the face is most expressive; the pasty white flesh has fine lines of black created by tiny feathers that produce an amusingly droll look. And there is a black bib under the face like the beard on a Smith Brothers Cough Drops ad.

Both of these species of macaws are mischievous, active, and bewitching. They make excellent pets. Certain individuals become good talkers, and one that has had good care makes an excellent additional member of the family, in most cases being passed on to the younger generation, because they usually outlive their original masters.

Macaws are now being bred in aviaries with considerable success, and Mrs. S. E. Guess of Atlanta has even succeeded in breeding a pair of her affectionate pets in a cage in her home, raising several nests from them.

Macaws thrive on the standard parrot diet described above for Amazon Parrots. In addition I find they appreciate dry bread, dog biscuits, and about once a week a fresh onion and a piece of pound cake. The day mine get onion I stay away!

Half-Moon Parrot

Another group of hookbills that finds its way into American homes is the conures, birds that might be described as smaller editions of the macaws. There is a large number of species in the genus and many of them are cagebirds, but only one is so common as to warrant inclusion in this volume, the Half-Moon (*Aratinga canicularis eburnirostrum*). It is also known as Petz' Conure and is sometimes sold as a "Miniature Parrot." It is about ten inches long, almost half tail. (See illustration, page 42.)

The Half-Moon is predominantly green, with some blue in flight feathers and a noticeable band of orange on the forehead. The crown is bluish. There is a large fleshy ring around the eye, yellowish in color.

A Half-Moon that has a small area of orange on the forehead is likely to be a young one and would likely become a splendid pet. Older ones may have learned bad habits (that may, in fact, be the reason why they are back on the market) and one ought to observe them to see how tame they appear to be, and how noisy. Half-Moons have a voice that can become offensive, and the time to evaluate the sound of it is before you ask the dealer to wrap it up for you. Feeding is the same as for Amazons.

Parrakeets

An unfortunate confusion exists in regard to the use of the term "parrakeet." Because of the overwhelming popularity of one species, the budgerigar, most people think of it when they encounter the term parrakeet. It is easy to understand why this happens, but it overlooks a sizeable group of fascinating birds of increasing popularity. The budgie is discussed later in the chapter on the "Well-Domesticated Birds and How To Breed Them."

But there are many other species of parrakeets that are kept as cagebirds. One of these is the Red-Rump Parrakeet (*Psephotus haematonotus*), an amiable and prolific Australian species. It has an unusual feature among hookbills, a musical whistle, to recommend it, and its pleasant disposition makes it an appropriate member of a mixed collection of finches, even when breeding.

The male's head, chest, and neck are green. The primary feathers of the wing are blue, as are also the shoulders, and the tail is green and blue. Underparts are yellow. And the rump is, of course, red. Females are more conservatively colored and the rump is green instead of red. Young birds are unusual in that their plumage indicates their sex from the time they are well feathered.

Red-Rump Parrakeet.

Another increasingly popular cagebird parrakeet is the Bourke's (*Neophema bourkii*). An unusual color pattern among hookbills, the Bourke's is brown with pastel rose and blue tones. His breast is a rosy pink, his thighs and rump blue, and some blue usually shows on the forehead. The female is quite similar, except that she lacks blue on the forehead.

Both the Bourke's and the Red-Rump are small enough to be called cagebirds. They breed readily in cages, and every year more fanciers are keeping them. They do well on a regular budgie feed mixture, plus some small sunflower seed.

Peachface Lovebird.

African Lovebirds

The African Lovebirds constitute another group of interesting cagebirds. They are now well enough established as domesticated species that they are readily available on the market.

Most of them are bright green over most of the body; all have stubby bodies, short tails, and strident voices. They are closely enough related that most of them will cross breed, and this has created the problem of mongrels in some carelessly managed aviaries.

The nesting habits are interesting. Lovebirds build their nests of strips of bark from tree branches, which they tear and chew to produce the proper softness. A two-inch piece is cut into an inverted V and is tucked under the rump feathers and carried to the nest. The nest has a long curved tunnel from the entrance to the egg cavity. I find a budgie nestbox to be the handiest nest for them (about 9″ × 9″ × 12″ high), although the lovebirds do not need the budgie's concave bottom. I have used fruit and mulberry branches successfully. I understand willow and eucalyptus are excellent, but I would avoid sappy trees like pines.

The most common species is the Peachface Lovebird (*Agapornis roseicollis*). In addition to the regular bright green body this species has a face of glorious peach color and a forehead of bright red. His rump is a bright blue and his tail has orange and black bands. The beak is coral. The Peachface is one of the larger of the common lovebirds, being about six inches long. Sexing is difficult. The female tends to be slightly larger than the male, but this is far from a reliable guide.

Probably second most common is the Masked Lovebird (*Agapornis personata*), a species slightly smaller and slightly less pugnacious than the Peachface. The body color is the same green but the head is black and the chest yellow. There is a bright red beak and large white fleshy rings around the eyes.

A mutant form is now firmly established and available in large numbers, the Blue Masked Lovebird. The body of the bird is blue rather than green, and white takes the place of yellow in the original. The beak is pink, rather than red. The Blue is certainly one of the prettiest of all lovebirds. For purposes of distinction it is usually referred to as Blue Masked Lovebird and the original as Black Masked Lovebird, but this is confusing. The "Blue" refers to the body color of the mutation and the "Black" refers to the color of the mask, which is the same in both color varieties. Not logical, but once you understand what is meant, it is a useful distinction. It would make more sense to refer to the original as the Green Masked Lovebird, but I have never heard anyone suggest it. Obviously, since it was named first (being the original) its naming did not comprehend the appearance of a blue variety later on.

Probably the third most common of the lovebirds in America is Fischer's Lovebird (*Agapornis fischeri*). A casual observer might confuse it with the Peachface, but not side by side. The Fischer's has a much more fiery shade of red on the head, and at the throat this merges to rose. The bill is red, the base of the tail bright blue, and there are fleshy rings around the eyes. Of the green lovebirds, this is my favorite.

Food is no problem with the lovebirds. I give mine budgie seed mixture plus small sunflower. They love to chew wood and have to have the wooden parts of their cages lined with metal, but they are attractive birds to keep and well worth the minor problems they present.

Lorikeets

Quite different in feeding habits from the other hookbills are the lorikeets. They are fascinating birds with irresistible mannerisms, and are becoming increasingly popular. Their main dietary ingredient is nectar, and they are equipped by nature with a specially adapted member for securing it, a brush-tipped tongue that enables them to lap up nectar as a cat does milk. They also eat fruit, and I have discovered that mine delight in a slice of bread moistened with milk and laced with fine threads of honey.

There are many species of lorikeets, but only two are commonly

Bourke's Parrakeet.

kept in this country. They are among the most colorful of all cagebirds, though, and when the authors of the leading American
publication on parrots selected a picture for the cover it was one
showing a pair of gorgeous Swainson's Lorikeets (*Trichoglossus
haematod moluccanus*), sometimes called the Blue Mountain Lorikeet or Rainbow Lorikeet. And few birds excel it for a color photo-
graph.

The Swainson's is about twelve inches long, and all beauty. The
basic body color probably should be identified as green, but the
other colors are so much more noticeable that they are the ones
one recalls. The head is purple with bright blue flecks. There is a
yellow collar dividing it from the rest of the body. The upper breast
varies from one bird to another, but all have a mixture of brilliant
red feathers with yellow, producing an unusual kind of orange.
The lower chest is a rich violet. Thighs are green, orange, and
yellow. The wing feathers have a unique band of yellow in the
center. The under-shoulder area is red and the extremities black.
The prominent hook-beak is a bright and shiny red. There is a

closely related species, the Red-Collared Lorikeet (*Trichoglossus haemotod rubritorquis*), which comes from the northern part of Australia rather than the Swainson's southern parts, and is identical except for the double collar, one of orange-red and one of blue.

Swainson's and Red-Collared breed fairly well in captivity, using large wooden nestboxes about 12″ × 12″ × 18″ high, but Dick Clarkson and Bill Wilson had a pair in Chicago that laid and incubated the clutch of eggs like a banty hen on the floor of an open pen in their busy bird showroom, oblivious of a stream of interested visitors.

One of the reasons for the popularity of the Swainson's is his personality. He is a mischievous bird, an acrobat, with most comic ways. He will prance to get attention, then go into the posture of a goose on parade, with head and neck almost vertical. Swainson's become tame very easily and soon will sit on the owner's hand. There is a problem of loose droppings because of the diet, but properly provided for, this is not a serious obstacle.

Talking Mynah

A few years ago I was admiring the season's crop of young canaries a friend had raised. She had them in a score of cages scattered about the house, and as we moved into the living room I heard a man's voice in the sunroom say, "Why, that's a thousand-dollar bird!" This roused my curiosity. I had heard of golden-throated singers, but this bird must be made of solid gold, I thought, as I edged to the sunroom. Much to my surprise no one was there. No one, that is, but a loquacious mynah with an incredible ability for conversation. He kept me speechless in amazement while he went on for a half hour of garrulous talk, hardly repeating himself more than my jovial barber would.

My friend told me she had not taught him that phrase. A visitor had said it to the bird in an impressive manner, and the bird had picked it up, repeated it, and it had become a permanent part of his tremendous vocabulary. And the price was really understated, she said. She had refused more than a thousand dollars for the bird. Just the week before, a convention of Ford Motor Company executives had met in Indianapolis. She had taken the bird to the banquet to perform on cue, but his impromptu remarks from the wings during the main speaker's speech disrupted things so hilariously that the affair was in an uproar. On one occasion they had to interrupt a TV program to explain that the wolf whistle in the background when a certain starlet came on the set had come not from one of the cameramen but from the mynah, and the camera had been turned on the bird to prove who the unmannerly culprit was.

Recently I was waiting for a friend in a pet shop that has its birds in a room separate from the rest of the store. I tried to enter the room unobtrusively so I could observe the birds in an unexcited state. As I paused at the threshold a very dulcet girl's voice said, "Hi, there." I looked around the room blankly, then heard a man's voice say, "Well, can't you answer me?" Then I saw a mynah looking at me with a friendly gleam in his eye.

There are many kinds of mynahs, but there is one imported for its talking qualities more than the others. It is the Indian Greater Hill Mynah (*Gracula religiosa*) and is not to be confused with other species if you want a talker. There are subspecies forms that differ slightly but talk well. Most of the better birds come from the Assam area or from the Himalayan mountain areas of Southeast Asia, hence the term "Hill" in the name.

If you are purchasing a young bird, it is important to get one as young as possible. Smoothness of plumage is not important at this stage; at best most babies are dull black and have messy, broken feathers from crowded conditions in the nursery where they have been kept. The things to look for are youthfulness and healthy vigor. Babies are usually imported when they are about six weeks old, before they are completely weaned, and if possible you should get yours right away. It is a nuisance to have to feed the baby by hand, but the years of pleasure to follow make it well worth the few weeks of bother until you wean him completely.

The bird should be fed on whatever the keeper has been giving him. Changing foods should always be gradual with any bird. The usual food is a dry mash to which moisture has been added either in the form of shredded vegetables (carrots, etc.) or liquid (milk or water). The food should be crumbly, not soggy. Keep some of the food in a dish in front of the bird so he will learn to eat on his own, but continue to push the food down his throat as long as he flutters his wings and gapes his mouth at you. The better you feed him, the better bird he will become, both in physical condition and in sociability. If the baby learns that human beings mean food, he comes to look on them as friends and never develops fearful attitudes.

Greater Hill Mynahs are omnivorous birds, that is, they will eat a wide variety of foods. It is wise to avoid fatty foods, however, since in captivity they have less opportunity to exercise than in the wild state. The best balanced diet appears to be a good Mynah Bird Food Mixture, which is available in any well-stocked pet shop, and plenty of fruit. Grapes are special favorites (cut in half if large), but banana, apple, pear, peach, etc., are welcome cut in pieces the size of a small grape. Fresh fruit is preferable, but when it is not available, canned fruit can be given—the lighter the syrup the better. In addition, such foods can be given as cooked potato, bread moistened with milk, moistened puppy meal, hard-cooked egg, cooked rice, pound cake, raw or cooked vegetables (hard ones grated), and a little raw or cooked beef a couple of times a week (preferably grated). *No bird seeds should be given.* If the preceding sounds as though feeding a mynah is complicated, I have erred. These are the many possibilities, not the requirements, of keeping a bird in good condition. The meal and fruit are basic; the other foods are frills and are not absolutely necessary.

Fresh drinking water should be available at all times, of course. Most mynahs like live food and the handiest food to offer is mealworms, purchased at a pet store. An occasional grasshopper in season will be appreciated. Ordinarily an adult mynah is fed once a day, but baby mynahs resemble human babies in needing a meal every few hours. A mature bird can be left over a weekend if plenty of food and water is provided. The problem is to find a food bowl heavy enough not to upset when the bird lands on it, yet small enough that it can be placed where droppings will not hit it and foul the food.

The worst problem when mynahs were first imported to this country was cleanliness. Because of the diet, the bird's droppings had a tendency to be jet-propelled across the room, and keeping the area clean was almost impossible. With the new dry foods the condition of the droppings has been much improved; they are more solid and more easily confined to the cage. Improved cages help, too. The new ones have a plastic guard around the sides and a wire bottom below which paper is placed on a drawer that slides out easily for quick and frequent changing. Keeping the bird smelling and looking pleasant is now simple.

Hill Mynahs enjoy a daily bath immensely and furnish an owner with great entertainment with their antics. This can be done by placing a shallow bowl of lukewarm water in the cage, but it is more of a treat to the bird to be given the freedom of the kitchen sink or bath tub, and it is easy to clean up afterward. A rubber mat may be needed so he will feel more secure on his feet. Sunbathing is a delight, too, as long as it is not too severe or too long.

A mynah can imitate different kinds of voices with complete fidelity. In a home where there are husband, wife, son, and daughter he will have four different voices when he reproduces what each teaches him. And if there is Fido, five.

An adult mynah in good condition is a handsome bird. His body size is about that of a banty chicken, although he does not have the erect posture. He is shiny jet black all over except for a brief white strip on each wing. He has a curious scallop of yellowish wattle on each cheek and in some cases running toward the back of the neck. This is a patch of bare skin that varies in size and distribution, depending on the particular valley in which the bird was hatched. The beak is a bright orange and the legs and feet yellow. And the head feathers look like a careful coiffure. They are neatly parted down the center, looking as though a fine-tooth comb had delicately settled them into place with tender precision, combing some to the right, the others to the left.

There is only a slight difference in appearance between the sexes, the male tending to have a more massive head, breast, and shoulders than the female, although this is a quality not simple to measure. The male also has a more noticeable bulge behind the eyes, seen best from above, and his pelvic bones are closer together. But the differences are relative and diagnosis is not certain. Talking qualities are not at all influenced by the sex of the bird.

The key to producing a talking mynah is the training process. One writer says humorously that to start with you have to be smarter than the bird. Fortunately for many of us, this is not true. All it takes is persistence. Those fanciers who have the greatest success try to set aside a period each day when the baby is taken into a quiet room for his lesson. This is usually explained as permitting the bird to learn habits of regularity and to bring him to concentrate on the lesson. I suspect the real function is to get the trainer to be regular and to concentrate, rather than the bird. But the system does seem to produce results regardless of which needs it most.

The first stage is to get the bird perfectly tame. If you get a "gaper" (a baby still being handfed), you can skip this stage. Otherwise you get him to become perfectly at ease in your presence, preferably on your arm. Then repeat to him patiently time and again the same phrase in the same tone of voice, without changing expression. Decide in advance the things you will want him to learn and for goodness sake, remember that he may repeat them when Aunt Mary or your pastor comes to visit. The first expression is the hardest one for him to learn. After he masters the technique of imitating human sounds he will learn additional phrases with increasing ease.

A few years ago I visited a place in California where there was a battery of about 50 cages, each containing a mynah and an amplifier hooked up to a tape recorder. The birds heard the same expressions all day long and were, I presume, pre-conditioned to repeat those phrases when they were sold. I never knew anyone who bought one of those babies so cannot report, but it makes sense that the birds would have been softened up to the sounds. Still, I think the personal attention of a particularly friendly human being would give better results. And I know it would do more for that particularly friendly human being.

Mynahs do not have the phenomenal life expectancy of parrots, but they do live to about fifteen years of age with good care. Thus it pays to get a baby and make him a member of the family. He will repay you many times over with his amusing antics and his lovable personality.

4

Well-Domesticated Birds
and How To Breed Them

M ANY OF THE BIRDS discussed in this book have been bred successfully in captivity. There are hundreds of ardent fanciers
in all parts of the world working at the challenge of breeding a species for the first time. The supreme test of an aviculturist's art is
his ability to reproduce natural conditions so well and to make his
charges so happy that they nest and raise their offspring. The
fancier who does this with a new species deserves great credit; he
has conquered problems no one has ever solved before, and avicultural societies award medals for such achievements.

Because scores of anonymous persons have worked at it for several years, it becomes possible for us to breed several species with
ease. The birds discussed in this chapter are thoroughly domesticated. All of the birds of these species now on the market have
been raised in captivity. No wild-trapped ones are available.

Canary

The oldest of the domesticated cagebirds is, of course, the
canary. The modern bird is the product of hundreds of generations

Orange Chopper Canary.

of breeding since that first wild bird from the Canary Islands was carried home by an unnamed Portuguese sailor of the Fifteenth Century. By the Seventeenth Century Italian, German, and English fanciers were raising them and writing about them.

The original ancestor from the Canary Islands and the neighboring area was a bird about five inches long, *Serinus canarius*. It is still to be seen on the islands, a yellowish bird with a great deal of brownish and gray tints. The wings are almost black and the abdomen and rump almost white. Beaks and legs are horn-colored with

Miniature Yorkshire Canary.

a tinge of pink at times. It is a bird far, far removed in appearance from the canaries seen on modern show benches.

Through selective breeding there have been developed more than a score of separate kinds of canaries, ranging from rollers and American Singers, bred purely for song qualities, to highly specialized body forms. There is the large Yorkshire, whose stately carriage and aristocratic shape give it the nickname of "Gentleman of the Fancy." There is the Dutch Frill, whose feathers swirl in all directions like an unpremeditated lace shawl. There is the Red Factor, which is bred for its fiery red color. There is the Lizard Canary, which is striped like a lizard. All of these and more have been produced by countless years of faithful bird management by fanciers with a dream toward which they strove.

Every seasoned canary fancier has his own system that works. The constantly amazing fact to me is that vigorous partisans of particular approaches to canariculture may be directly contradictory in their positions, each insisting that his system is the best. Bird clubs are great debating societies.

The canary-breeding procedures described here are those favored by most fanciers, simplified for the beginner. But it is a system I have tested; I am writing this in the midst of breeding season and am using the approach I outline, with minor exceptions.

It is pointless to try to breed unless the birds are in breeding condition. This is noted when the male is in full song and acts enthusiastic about it. Characteristically, he prances while he is singing, and sings much of the time. In general, the condition of the males parallels the hens', and if the hens are coming into condition, the cocks are also ready.

The hen is a little more easily recognized as ready for mating. She tears paper and carries it in her beak, flits restlessly about the cage, stretches her wings fitfully as if indecisive about flying, and calls to the males. Her abdomen swells like a ripe melon, although this is not too sure a sign if you do not know how it looks before she comes into condition. This can be seen by holding her upside down and blowing the feathers away from the vent.

The male usually finishes his fall moult and begins singing sometime around October. If you have not separated the sexes earlier, it should be done at this time. The female ignores him because she ordinarily has no interest in breeding until January or later. An old rule of thumb had fanciers putting their pairs together on February 14th—Valentine's Day.

One male can successfully serve two females. This is the system I use. I use double breeders, canary cages about eighteen inches long with a channel in the center for a divider to be inserted. I put two of them end-to-end, with the door between open so the male can pass from cage to cage. After inserting the dividers I put two hens on the outside ends, the cock in the middle so he can feed either hen through the divider. When a hen has apparently accepted him I remove the divider so they can mate, and give her a nest and nesting material, after having closed the door between the two cages. I allow him to run with one hen, then the other, for part of each day, merely removing the wire netting separating the cages at his doorway long enough for him to hop through (but not a hen). In this way it is not necessary to catch a bird at all.

After the fourth egg is laid I move the cages to a quiet place and let the hen set alone. The usual clutch is four or five eggs. Thirteen days after she has started to set the eggs should hatch. Some fanciers insist that the first two eggs should be removed from the nest, restored when the fourth is laid. The reason is to have all hatch at the same time so the older babies will not have an unfair advantage over the younger ones, crowding them out at feeding time. Other fanciers insist that this is unnecessary. You can take your pick, but if you remove the eggs, be sure to turn them several times, as the mother does, to encourage circulation. I belong to the don't-remove-them school, and rarely have a starved runt in the nest.

Sometimes the thirteen days of incubation stretch a day or two, so do not become impatient. The hen may have delayed setting in earnest. While she is setting, avoid disturbing her as much as possible. Keep fresh water and food before her, but do not bother her otherwise.

When the babies are about eighteen days old, they will be fully

Orange Chopper Canary.

feathered and a few days later will leave the nest for the first (and usually the last) time. The hen will be thinking about nesting again and if she shows such interest the male can be reintroduced to the cage and left with her. He usually will not bother the babies, and often will take over some fatherly feeding duties. Courtship may become rather violent, with the male chasing the female while he sings loudly. This is normal procedure and if she does not fight back there is nothing to worry about.

When the babies are seen to be feeding themselves, they can be removed. It is important to continue the same soft food and to be

Ringneck Parrakeets (male on left).

sure all are eating. It is a good idea not to have perches in the cage the babies are moved to; they must be close to the food.

All kinds of elaborate diets have been promoted by fanciers, but the simplest one I have ever heard is also the best I have ever used and is completely satisfactory. I grate a hard-cooked egg, add to it about an equal amount of cornflake crumbs purchased in a dispenser box at the supermarket, and toss the two ingredients with a fork to mix. And I give all the fresh lettuce the bird wants, sometimes an amazing amount. I have never had plumper babies than those raised on this simple formula.

For those who have only one hen to a cock (and this is really preferable to the arrangement I described), the system is much simpler. Leave the male with the hen all the time. He will not distract her while she is setting, and will take over much of the feeding job, especially if she lays again before the babies are weaned.

It is desirable to place seamless bands on the babies. This is done when they are about a week old, depending on their size. The three forward toes together are threaded through the band, then the band is pushed up the leg until the fourth toe (like a thumb) is released. The band then is loose on the leg. After the baby is older the band cannot come off, and it provides absolute identification of the bird, including age. Each band is numbered and there are no two alike. Bands are for sale through bird clubs or from manufacturers who advertise in bird magazines.

Budgie or Parrakeet

More numerous than the canary in this country is the budgerigar (*Melopsittacus undulatus*), commonly called the parrakeet. This bewitching fellow has won the hearts of millions of families and brings joy to countless lonely persons. The Public Health Service estimates that there are between ten and fifteen million budgies in this country, which equals one for every other family. Entire colonies of them exist in the wild in California and the Florida Keys, as well established as native birds.

Budgies are easily raised. When in breeding condition the fleshy portion on the upper beak, the cere, turns a rich brown in the female and a bright blue in the male. No nest is built, but the bottom of the nestbox should be concave. Most pet shops carry budgie nestboxes about six inches square and ten inches high, with a two-inch entrance hole and a round hollowed-out space on the bottom about a half inch deep and about three inches in diameter. This serves to gather the eggs so the hen can incubate them without one straying into a cold corner.

The hen lays from four to six white eggs on alternate days and incubates them about eighteen days. Since she may have started incubating before laying the last egg, some eggs may hatch before others, and the babies, being larger, get more of the food, but this is usually not a serious problem. No supplementary food is really required, although what is on the market is good to use. The parents can raise healthy babies on their usual diet of white millet and canary seed. They also need grit, greenfood, fruit, and fresh water daily.

At the age of five weeks babies are perfect for finger-taming. They will have been out of the nest and eating on their own for a few days. Some fanciers clip the wings by snipping six or eight feathers from one wing, a perfectly painless operation. By leaving the outside three primary feathers untouched the bird is not visibly disfigured, and by clipping only one wing the baby is enabled to break a fall but not to fly with any degree of confidence. This steadies him much quicker and he becomes tame enough to sit on one's finger more readily than if he is free to fly away. After his first moult, his feathers grow back in and he has complete mobility unless you repeat the trimming, but by then he will fly to you from any part of the house.

Budgies occur in almost endless series of colors. In the wild they are green with yellow faces, but through careful breeding a large number of other colors have been produced, including violet, sky blue, gray, snow white, and most of the shades in between.

The current dream of many budgie specialists is to breed a red budgie. The first one will be worth thousands of dollars. Last year I thought I had found the pot at the end of the rainbow. While wandering up a side street in Madrid, Spain, I came across a wizened old man selling blue budgies that had not the characteristic white foreheads, but all six of them, male and female, had bright red foreheads. The find of a lifetime! I got his asking price— only a dollar or two a piece—then asked how he had obtained these birds. "Simple," he replied. Reaching into the box on his bicycle he drew out a bottle and a fine brush. "I paint them whatever color pleases me. This week it was red." There went my dream of fame and fortune.

Cockatiel

Another parrot-family bird that is very easy to breed is the cockatiel (*Leptolophus hollandicus*). Although originally an Australian bird, all of the cockatiels now on the market are the result of many generations of cage- or aviary-breeding.

The cockatiel is a beautiful and impressive bird. He is about 13 inches long, slender and stately in posture. Although his basic colors are gray and white, one is impressed most by the striking bright yellow crest, which is usually carried erect, the large orange spot

Mature opaline budgie
(note lack of neck markings).

about the size of a dime on each cheek, and the bright yellow forehead and throat. The cockatiel is a colorful bird. Hens and young males are noticeably less brilliant in their head colors, but the pattern is similar.

One of the main advantages of the cockatiel is his absolute peacefulness. I have never known one to fight with anything. Even small finches and waxbills are safe in the same cage. And this placid disposition makes the cockatiel an ideal family pet, also. There are many families that have enlarged the circle to include a

Mature male cockatiel.

cockatiel that participates in all the activities from the breakfast table to the 11:00 p.m. TV newscast. Some learn to talk, but their ability is usually limited.

Care of the cockatiel is a simple matter. The usual budgie seed mixture plus small sunflower seed does well for the basic diet. A little greenfood and fruit, grit, and water complete the menu, with an occasional treat of hemp seed. On this simple diet they rear healthy and vigorous babies.

There are various systems used by fanciers to raise cockatiels. The easiest way is to turn a few pairs loose in a large room, install nestboxes, and let nature take its course. I have seen this done and it works. But for the fancier with limited space the Cockatiel will breed in a cage, too. The larger the cage, the better, but I have bred them in one 30″ long, 18″ high, and 15″ deep, with the nestbox mounted on the outside of the cage.

The most popular nestbox is about 12″ square and 24″ deep, with a 3″ hole, but the birds are tolerant and will accept many variations. Some fanciers furnish no nesting material but give a concave bottom to the box, as described for budgies. Others put about 4″ of decayed wood in the bottom of the box and permit the birds to construct their own bowl. I have always thought this would make it easy to keep the eggs moist and thus avoid the problem of chicks dead in a tough shell, but since I never have the problem in my birdroom, which is naturally damp enough, I have never tried it. I use the bare box quite satisfactorily.

A clutch is usually about six eggs which are incubated for eighteen days. A good pair may raise as many as three full broods in a season—eighteen lively offspring—but more than three such nests should be discouraged by removing the nestbox to allow the parents to recoup their energy.

Two mutant forms have appeared, the albino and the pied. The former is still extremely rare. The latter is becoming increasingly available, and some of the specimens are gorgeously marked. There is no predicting what the color pattern of offspring will be, because some of the cream-colored splotches may appear on almost any part of the body.

The cockatiel deserves his growing popularity and can be expected to find his way into an ever increasing number of homes. He has all the charm and personality of the budgie, plus a strong additional appeal to those who love the exotic.

Zebra Finch

The Zebra Finch (*Taeniopygia castanotis*) is an irresistible combination of color, sound, and personality. Of the scores of species I have kept over the years, the Zebra is the one I always come back to as my favorite. If they were not so easily raised, Zebras would be so sought after that the price would skyrocket. Fortunately, they are thoroughly domesticated and the supply is plentiful.

A male Zebra Finch is handsome indeed. About the size of our domestic wren, he sports a surprising assortment and arrangement of colors. The most prominent feature is his huge cherry-red beak that glistens as if it were waxed and polished. On each cheek is a large round burnt-orange spot like the cheek of a Dutch doll. His flanks are chestnut, spotted with many tiny cream polka dots. Other upper parts are a soft gray. Fine horizontal pencilings lace the upper breast, getting thicker and thicker until they merge in a wide black cummerbund that divides the chest from the abdomen. The tail has broad black and white bars. Under each diminutive sparkling black eye is a black comma that looks like a permanent tear drop. Here is more creative use of color per gram than anyplace else I know.

But appearance is not the Zebra's only attraction. He is the nearest thing to perpetual motion ever to wear feathers. His rate of metabolism must be tremendous. Always on the move, hardly ever still, he punctuates his movements with an indescribable piping reminiscent of a tin horn for New Year's Eve, carefully muted. But when he is frightened or excited, the volume and pitch rise so much that I use Zebras as watchdogs. I can always tell when a bird is loose in my birdroom by the higher-pitched, frantic calls of the Zebras, who shout the alarm whenever anything strange happens. I have been saved serious accidents on several occasions when, alerted by the Zebras, I have found a bird caught in the wire, a cat at the window, or a cageful of birds flying freely in the room because I forgot to latch the door.

The song and dance of the Zebra is a fascinating performance. He thrusts his chest forward, stretches his neck like a giraffe, sticks all his feathers out perpendicularly from his body like a porcupine, and hops up and down rhythmically, all the while mincing a ludicrous variation of a tin-horn symphony. This performance takes place frequently, but the female acts as if she does not know the

Gray Zebra Finch (male is at left).

male exists. When he crowds her too closely, she calmly seeks another perch, hardly deigning to recognize his presence in the same cage with her.

There is no specific breeding season for Zebras, but they do breed better during the lengthening spring days and the warm summer nights. However, last winter we had several nests of Zebra babies hatch in an unheated flight while the temperatures did not get above ten degrees below zero for two weeks, and we did not lose a chick. The water dishes froze over within a half hour, but the birds remained happy and active. And prolific!

I raise Zebras both in individual cages and in colonies and both systems have their advantages. The easiest way is to turn several pairs loose in a flight and let them sort out their own mates. If you want to control the colors, you can put all of one color in a flight. For strict control of heredity it is necessary to breed in cages and only one pair to a cage. The cage does not have to be large. I have used canary double-breeder cages (10″ × 10″ × 18″ long).

The nestbox most breeders use is 5 inches cubed, with the front half open. This small box discourages the favorite vice of Zebra Finches, "egg sandwiches." When you are cleaning out a Zebra nestbox, it is not at all unusual to find five layers of nesting material, each layer separated from the adjoining layer by a clutch of second-hand eggs. The Zebra is a real home-builder and enjoys nothing quite so much as building a nest, even if it means he must build on top of the eggs in the present nest. There is no way to prevent this in a flight, where scraps and feathers are always available. In an individual cage it can be discouraged by withholding all forms of temptation, but this means not even paper on the floor of the cage.

The best nesting material I have found is burlap yarn. I wash a burlap seed sack, cut it into two-inch squares, then unravel it. This provides a bulky material that is warm, absorbent, sanitary, and easily obtained. Longer lengths should be avoided, because of the danger of the bird's becoming entangled.

If the birds are in top breeding condition, they are not nearly so likely to be diverted from serious incubation. The hen will lay from four to eight white pea-sized eggs and set for about two weeks.

Male Pied Fawn Zebra Finch.

In another two weeks the babies will start trying to leave the nest and in two more weeks will be weaned, at which time "mom" is likely to have another clutch of eggs well on the way. The babies are colored like the mother—plain gray and white, with a few black markings here and there—except that their beaks are black instead of pale orange.

Young Zebras mature quickly. I had always found it hard to accept at face value Mr. Edward J. Boosey's statement that he had known Zebra Finches six weeks old to reproduce, but one summer I put some Zebras in a flight before I left home in June for an extensive trip (during which I visited Mr. Boosey in England), and when I got back in September, I had the third generation in the nest! Could the Jukes or Kallikaks beat that record?

One of the reasons why Zebra Finches have become so popular is their several mutant forms. The one described is the original, known as the Normal or Gray form. But there are now several other color varieties well established, some of which have tremendously interesting hereditary patterns. A booklet published several years ago to list the possible hereditary combinations ran to about sixty pages of fine print, and even more mutant forms have appeared since then.

The commonest mutation is the White Zebra, a dazzling pure snow white. The only other colors are the cherry red beak, pink legs, and black eyes. Hens have less brilliant beaks. There is also the Fawn Zebra Finch, formerly also called Cinnamon. He has all the markings described for the Normal Gray except that the gray is replaced by a soft brownish tone.

Even when crossed these three color varieties produce birds that always look like one or the other of the parents, never a combination of traits. But there is a separate mutant form that does combine the pure white and normal markings, the Chestnut-Flanked White Zebra. The cock has a white body but he has the fine Zebra-like lines on the breast, the tear drop under the eye, the large orange cheek spots, and the polka-dotted chestnut flanks. Hens are white except for the tear drop.

The Gray Penguin Zebra Finch is a somewhat lighter gray than the Normal, to which is added also a lacewing effect caused by a lighter shade of delicate gray edging each tiny feather on the wings. This does not show to best advantage until after the bird has moulted twice. He has no trace of chest-barring, the chest and abdomen being white. Cheek patches are pale orange or cream. Other markings are as in the Normal Gray. The Penguin markings can be bred into the other color varieties, also.

There is another mutant trait that produces beautiful varieties, the Dilute. This can be bred in all the varieties except white, where it is invisible. It has the effect of reducing the depth of the color of the bird, so that the dilute form of the Gray Zebra is called Silver or, sometimes, Blue. And I think the most beautiful of all the Zebras is the Cream, which is the dilute form of Fawn. There is a softness of tone in the very light beige of this color variety that places him at the top of my list.

One other mutant form should be mentioned, the Pied. This appears in all colors except the white, and it consists of irregular and unpredictable splotches of white on all parts of the body. A well-marked Pied Zebra is a pretty bird. The challenge in bird shows is to enter a pair whose white markings are as nearly identical as possible.

Because of this tendency to mutate new forms, there is an additional fascination to the raising of Zebra Finches. This was one of the reasons for the explosion in popularity of budgies, and it accounts in part for the booming interest in Zebras. Some of these traits are recessive, some dominant. Some are sex-linked, which means that the hereditary trait is passed on in its hidden form only from mother to son, never from mother to daughter. Because many of these hereditary traits are carried in hidden form from generation to generation, all kinds of crazy-quilt patterns of inheritance are possible, and if you have two birds whose ancestry you do not know, you may get a half-dozen different colors among their offspring.

Last year I had a baby White Zebra whose feathers would not lie down no matter how much she preened them. She looked very unkempt and I was disgusted with her, but I had no way of disposing of her, so I tossed her into a flight with a lot of other birds and forgot about her. I suppose I saw her a hundred times in the next few months, but it was not until she was about a year old and had matured into a fuzzy ball of ostrich-like plumes that the light went on in my mind and I realized that, to my knowledge, I had the first Frilled Zebra.

I have no way of knowing now whether she is a mutation or a sport (whether she can pass on to her offspring the frilled trait or whether it is a mere disarray of plumage that will end with her) but I am attempting to find out. She is an amusing sight and if she is properly line-bred to improve the appearance, her progeny will be quite a novelty. And this constant challenge of new varieties among Zebras is one of the traits accounting for the great popularity of this fascinating species.

Bengalese or Society Finch

Another domesticated bird of great appeal is the Bengalese or Society Finch (*Uroloncha domestica*), probably the most easily bred of all foreign birds. The Bengalese never existed as a wild bird; it is the result of centuries of breeding by skilled Oriental aviculturists who crossed various species to produce this entirely new one. The origins are buried in mystery, but it appears that the an-

Male Brown and White Society Finch in courting dance.

cestry includes the Striated Finch (*Munia striata*), the Indian Silverbill (*Euodice malabarica*), and the Sharp-Tailed Finch (*Munia striata acuticauda*).

The modern Bengalese (sometimes called Bengalee in the singular) is about two-thirds the size of a canary. There are two quite common varieties and two less common.

Most frequently seen is the chocolate-and-white Bengalese, a mottled pattern of dark brown and white, with no two birds having the same distribution of colors.

Next in numbers is the fawn-and-white, which is a lovely shade of soft sand-yellow scattered unpredictably on white. The surprising fact is that when a fawn is mated to a chocolate, the offspring are either fawn or chocolate, sometimes both occurring in the same nest, but no one bird displays both chocolate and fawn feathers. One of the challenges on the show bench is to get a pair in which both birds have the same markings, but this almost never is done perfectly.

A pure white variety exists, also. This is not an albino, which

Fawn and White Society Finch.

would have pink eyes. I never heard of a true albino Bengalese. The white variety that exists has a constitutional weakness that produces cataracts in older birds, and many whites go blind when they are two or three years old. If blind ones are kept in the cage to which they are accustomed, they get along satisfactorily, even reproducing in some cases, because they know the layout of the cage and can find food, water, and nest.

The newest mutant variety is the Self, occurring in both chocolate and fawn. The Chocolate Self is solid chocolate, without white, and the Fawn Self is similar, but the fawn makes a particularly pretty bird.

Rare among cagebirds other than the canary is the crested form, which can be found in all colors. The Bengalese crest is the kind termed "rosette" by canary breeders: a circular crest in which feathers radiate from the center of the top of the head, like spokes of a wheel. A perfect crest is smooth, with unbroken regularity, and these tend to come from pairs where one parent is crested and the other is not. When two crested birds are mated to each other, the offspring tend to have crests broken with bald patches.

Bengalese are such dependable breeders that they are used by the thousands in Japan, where their main function is to be foster parents for the more rare finches, who usually make unsatisfactory parents. A Japanese aviculturist may have a few pairs of Star Finches, Lady Goulds, Shaft-Tails, or Parrot Finches, then scores of pairs of Bengalese. As the rare birds lay, their eggs are placed under Bengalese, where they are raised with a much higher degree of success.

Breeding habits are quite similar to those already described for the Zebra Finch. Bengalese have the same virtues, the same vices, and use the same equipment. They feed on the same mixture and require the same treatment in general. The only difference is a slight preference among Zebras for aviary over cage, and a slight preference by Bengalese in the opposite direction.

Lady Gould or Gouldian Finch

The most garishly colored of all the finches is the Lady Gould or Gouldian Finch (*Poephila gouldiae*). The extreme variation in colors, their abrupt separation from one another, and their brilliance well explain the reaction of a friend of mine when he saw his first Lady Gould cock, "I don't believe it." If we were to see such a gaudily colored bird on a dime store plaque, we would reject it as overdone. It is easy to understand why the famous naturalist John Gould named the finch after his wife when he first found the bird in Australia.

The Gould is about the size of a canary. His upper parts are bright green, his rump sky blue, his chin and upper throat jet black, his upper breast a rich purple, and the lower breast canary yellow. Delicate lines of black and turquoise separate the bright red face from the green neck. Legs are a fleshy pink and in full breeding condition the beak is light pink set off with a bright red tip, as if he had just had a sip of red ink. The two central tail feathers come to a long and delicate point. Females are colored in a similar pattern but the shades are markedly subdued. Sexing adult birds is no problem.

Two other color varieties exist, but the only difference is in the color of the head. The one described above is referred to as Red-Headed Lady Gould Finch. There are also the Black-Headed and the Yellow-Headed, the latter being more orange than yellow. I note a tendency to downgrade the beauty of the Black-Headed, but I find him fully as gorgeous as his counterparts.

The breeding pattern of the three colors is convenient in that crossing the colors, which can be done without any difficulty as far as the birds are concerned, never produces a mixture of the color varieties in the plumage of the babies. The offspring may include all three colors in the same nest but each baby will look like a pure type (although he may be quite mixed genetically).

Lady Goulds are fully domesticated, and there is no danger of our losing the supply, although Australian law now makes it illegal to trap them. There are, however, a few problems associated with their culture that seem to keep the supply limited.

It has never seemed logical to me, but the fact appears to be that many Lady Goulds prefer to nest in our winter months, which are the summer months in Australia. Everything I know tells me this ought not to be true, but most of the Lady Gould fanciers I know

*Four variations of the Society Finch. Foreground, left to right:
Brown and White, White-Crested, White; rear: Brown and White.*

report that their birds come into breeding condition in late fall
and are busiest during the depth of our winter in the Northern
Hemisphere. Someone has suggested that we keep calendars out
of sight so that when the Gould sees the December leaf come up
he won't get ideas. I question whether the Gould really can read,
though. Perhaps it is the calendar pictures that set him off. Whatever the cause, he is most active in our winter. But canary fanciers
are accustomed to having birds nest while the snow is deep outside
the doorway, so perhaps the Lady Gould is not too erratic.

As he comes into condition, the male begins his courtship in a manner that is highly persuasive to a female Gould but
hardly to anyone else. He sits back a bit more nearly erect on the
perch, extends his neck like a boy soprano reaching for a high note,
and "sings." That word has to be put in quotation marks because
it is hardly accurate. The "song" can barely be heard six feet away,
which is no great disadvantage because it consists of a sound resembling the rubbing of two pieces of sandpaper together ever so

Red-Headed Lady Gould (male).

gently. If you have a friend who wants a bird but cannot stand a noisy canary, the Lady Gould is the answer. The male never would intrude on his peace.

This reminds me of a letter I got from a reader of my column in *American Cage-Bird Magazine* one time asking in all seriousness if we ought not to refer to the male of this species as the Lord Gould Finch! I never have figured out a suitable reply to that question.

Fanciers succeed with breeding the Goulds both in aviaries and in cages. Although for maximum production some aviculturists, particularly the Japanese, prefer to have the Goulds lay the eggs but not waste time incubating them or raising the babies (which are raised by Society Finches instead), the Goulds are fully capable of performing the complete operation.

Baby Lady Goulds have several phosphorescent nodules in their mouths that look like tiny beacons to enable the parents to find the bottomless cavern. Some pairs are amazingly prolific, raising a succession of sturdy youngsters each year. The crucial stage appears to be the first moult, at which time the rather drab green young birds experience some difficulty and some do not survive.

Lady Goulds build their own nests out of grasses, fine rootlets, burlap twine, and similar materials. They usually prefer the standard small finch nestbox (5″ × 5″ × 5″, with the front half open) or the globular wicker baskets now on the market. They incubate the eggs and feed the young with fair dependability, but fortunate indeed is the fancier who has a number of Zebra Finches or Bengalese in the same stage of family-rearing cycle if needed as foster parents for neglected eggs or babies of Lady Goulds.

Goulds have acquired a reputation for frailty that is not entirely deserved. I do not know why, but one morning a bird will be vigorous and appear perfectly healthy but in the evening be dead. On one occasion I imported six pairs from Japan. They were large, gorgeous birds in excellent condition. Within two months all were dead and not one had appeared to be in ill health for a moment.

This trait leads to considerable discussion as to their care. There are numerous theories, two of which I observe just to play safe but without much conviction. One is that the Goulds must have access to rock salt and the other is that they need finely crushed cuttlebone at all times. In addition I give mine the usual assortment of grit, greens, fruit, whole cuttlebone and plenty of fresh water.

Food is simple. They take the ordinary finch mixture, to which I usually add a little niger (black thistle) when they are breeding. I offer them commercial egg-food mixtures and the egg-and-cornflake-crumb food described for nesting canaries, but some pairs accept it and others do not. I offer milk-moistened bread to those who seem to want it, too. I have never had much success feeding them mealworms, but a friend who has twenty pairs in a large flight has his eating large amounts of live mealworms and various food supplements.

White and Ringneck Doves

The cagebirds that come nearest to being indestructible are the Ringneck Dove and his popular variation, the White Dove, sometimes called Sacred Dove. They thrive under most adverse conditions and a breeding pair will continue to produce offspring with almost monotonous regularity until you have run out of friends to give them to.

Originally the Ringneck came from India, but it has been cage-bred for so many years that what we now have are all perfectly domesticated. Occasionally the White Dove is sold as a Ceylon Dove.

The Ringneck is a bird of quiet beauty. He is soft fawn all over except for a black band almost encircling the neck. The better White Doves are pure white, but most birds have a faint suggestion of a collar. Both forms are large for cagebirds, about nine inches long, but their amiable nature makes them ideally suited to mixed collections, and since they tend to be fairly inactive they do adequately in enclosures ordinarily too small for such large birds. They do not need heat in winter if there is a shelter into which they can retreat from storms. Sexing is not easy but in general the female is smaller, has a flatter head, is more delicately constructed, and has a wider space between her pelvic bones. The courting display of the male is unmistakable and is positive proof of sex.

Most doves are peaceful around other birds, but they tend to be pugnacious toward other doves. I have never seen Ringnecks or Whites commit mayhem even on others of the same species, however. They may fight over nesting sites and break eggs, but they are not likely to cause damage to each other.

On one occasion I was puzzled by finding four of my Ringnecks literally scalped, heads bleeding from picking on each other, I assumed. I watched the flight to see why this un-dovelike behavior and was surprised to see a budgie descend on a startled dove and ride around piggy-back while he dug into the poor thing's lacerated

Ringneck Dove.

White Dove.

Diamond Doves (male on left).

Male Button Quail eating mealworm.

head. I suppose the dove weighed five times as much as the budgie but he was unable to defend himself.

These doves are easily cared for. They will eat almost any kind of grain they are offered, consuming it whole. If they are in a mixed collection of hardbills I let them eat whatever the others are getting. If alone I give them millet or budgie mixture. They breed readily, building a flimsy nest of twigs in which two white eggs are laid. The male incubates from mid-morning to mid-afternoon, the female the rest of the time. Babies are fed on regurgitated liquid ("pigeon milk") by both parents, who pump the fuzzy little fellows full until their crops look distorted. No change in food is needed when they are feeding babies.

The coo of the Ringneck or the White Dove is a beautiful sound. I like to keep at least one pair around for this reason. But usually two birds have a way of becoming four, four becoming eight, eight becoming sixteen, and by then all I can hear is doves.

Diamond Dove

Somewhat smaller than the preceding species, the Diamond Dove (*Geopelia cuneata*) is the smallest dove commonly kept. It is only about seven inches long and most of that is tail. The overall color is bluish gray, with white at the vent. The striking features are the spectacles created by the large, pink, fleshy cere around the eyes and the sparkling white spots that speckle the wings. The male tends to have more of these than the female and is generally larger and bolder in his build and manner.

But the male delights at showing off, and if there is one present in a group of Diamond Doves he is sure to reveal his gender by throwing his head in the air, then low to the ground, meanwhile puffing out his throat and spreading his colorful tail like a peacock. His coo is a delightfully high-pitched one and it comes out with a determined tone. I am always reminded of a banty rooster when I see a Diamond Dove display.

For nesting they like a platform about five inches square and an inch deep, or an open box like a small shelf-cage. After building an unstable nest of grasses, small twigs, and whatever else they can find, they lay two white eggs and incubate for about two weeks. The babies are fed on regurgitated seed in liquid form. A prolific pair will raise several nests a season. All the Diamond Doves now available are cage- or aviary-bred, since Australia has banned commercial exportation of native birds.

Diamond Doves are absolutely peaceful around even the tiniest of waxbills but two breeding pairs of Diamonds should not be placed together. They feed on millet or ordinary budgie or finch mixtures and do not need other food when feeding babies. In winter they need shelter but not heat.

Button Quail

Another miniature that is small enough to be regarded as a cagebird is the Button Quail (*Excalfactoria chinensis*), often called Chinese Painted Quail. It is a charming bird that gives one the impression that it is a dwarf Bob-White Quail. It is a round little thing only about four inches long, with brown body, white and black face, chestnut underparts and blue-gray breast. The hen is noticeably less colorful, being various shades of brown all over.

The Button Quail is native to a broad expanse of Southeast Asia, but most sold on the United States market have been hatched here. Although some hens raise their own broods in a planted aviary, many lay their eggs profusely and at random around the aviary. Breeding Button Quail prefer aviaries in which there is long grass. The hen hollows out a spot on the ground and deposits eight or nine eggs in it. As soon as they hatch the babies are able to run around, looking like little brown marbles. Some fanciers have good results feeding them egg food similar to that given breeding canaries. The babies also relish live ants' cocoons when they are offered.

Adult Button Quail eat any of the seed mixtures ordinarily fed cagebirds. They will clean up the food spilled from hoppers hung on the wall, but because they stay on the ground it is important that some food be on that level for them. They winter outside readily as long as there is shelter into which they can retreat from storms. They never bother a perching bird so are completely safe to place even with the tiniest of finches. If the aviary does not provide it, a box of dry sand a few inches deep will be appreciated for bathing purposes.

The birds discussed in this chapter afford their owners the additional joy of watching a perfectly happy pet manifest his contentment by setting up housekeeping and raising a family. Colorful birds are pretty to look at, singing birds are lovely to listen to, but these highly domesticated ones add another dimension by allowing the fancier to share with them the delights of parenthood. No pet ever "belongs" to you quite so much as the one you watched develop from the first piece of yarn carried about in the mother's mouth as she looked for a nest. This is the supreme delight of the aviculturist.

Black-Crested Finch (Pygmy Cardinal), a popular South American finch with a soft song.

5

General Care and Management

ENCLOSURES FOR BIRDS RANGE from a simple home-made cage of hardware cloth to an elaborate walk-in flight of concrete and glass. You are limited only by imagination, space, and pocketbook. A little planning in advance will be repaid in attractiveness, convenience, and economy, so careful consideration of all the possibilities is advisable.

Cages

There is a wide range of cages produced for the commercial market, and you can find almost anything you want by shopping around. Unfortunately, many of the manufacurers know more about the furnishings market than they do about birds, and the cages they produce are completely inadequate.

The cage that is broader at the top than at the bottom may be ideal for designers' pictures in a woman's magazine, but the droppings will land on the damask sofa under the cage, not on the diminutive floor of the cage. A cage that is tall and narrow might almost as well be short and narrow. The bird needs lateral space more that vertical. Perches should not be placed over each other, nor over feed or water dishes. Spaces between wires should *never* be V-shaped, getting narrower toward the bottom; this makes a perfect guillotine for a bird that lands on the wire, sticks his head through, then slides down to his death.

If you are looking for a large cage for a mixed collection, it may be wise to start with a "finch spacing" cage, one with ⅜-inch space between the wires. Canary and budgie spacing is ⅝ inch. The cages sold as "finch spacing" will hold the tiniest of birds (Orange-Breasted Waxbills, Strawberry Finches, etc.), but the little fellows will go through a canary or budgie cage when they are frightened.

Many cages offer an option of covered or uncovered seed and water cups, the former having a hood over the dish. Although they are less attractive, I prefer the covered ones for sanitary reasons. In general metal cages are preferable to bamboo cages, too, because soiled portions can be washed without stains remaining. In case of infection, a metal cage is easily immersed in a disinfectant solution. There are good commercial disinfectant products on the market, but I find any of the common chlorine liquid bleaches in a laundry tub of water, following the directions on the label, to be quite satisfactory.

For those who make their own cages, a number of simple aids make it easy. If you want a number of collapsible cages that fold flat for easy storage, they can be made by cutting flat sheets of netting in desired sizes and fastening them together at the corners with wire or metal fasteners manufactured for this purpose and sold with special pliers through farm outlets or small livestock magazines. These clips hold securely but are loose enough so that they serve like hinges, permitting you to fold the sheets. Wire can be made to perform the same function. Doors for these cages can easily be cut and hinged in the same manner. I find the handiest fastener of all to be the old-fashioned spring clothespin, which is handy to open or close with one hand even though the other hand is holding a bird or a dish. If you must be modern, you can find spring clothespins in brightly colored plastic, but keep them away from parrots. They splinter quickly and are digested slowly.

The system just described for constructing collapsible cages also works quite well for permanent cages. I have learned through aggravating experience never to build a round cage, even though they are the easiest kind to make with this method, because I hate to cut out discs from old newspapers to fit the bottom of the round cage. And I have also learned that it saves hours of time over the years if I construct the cage to fit our local newspaper. Thus I can lay down several layers of paper in a clean cage, then remove the top sheet or two daily to preserve a neat appearance. If the paper fits, it is really quite effortless to do this.

In building or remodeling, a fertile imagination may come up with striking ideas for building live birds into the decor. One lovely home I saw had a mixed collection in the entry hall. Rather than exposing the birds to drafts from the open door, the owner had a sheet of plate glass as the cage front. For ventilation he installed plastic egg-crate material that is used for fluorescent lighting, then hung the lights over the huge cage. If the species are not too excitable this works out well, but too nervous kinds of birds will keep the glass messy.

Some creative fanciers use cages for room dividers, building in a large cage between living and dining rooms or as a part of the family room. These can easily be planted cages, with tough potted plants that can withstand rough treatment from birds and poor sunlight. A number of years ago we made our front porch into a room to adjoin the living room, and rather than plaster over the hole where the window was, I built in a large cage, surrounded it with gilt picture molding, and put a portrait light over it. It makes a living picture and always is a conversation piece. I think we had the most delightful results with it when we had a vivacious hummingbird in it, and we put in a large blooming plant of cattleya orchids. The orchids exude considerable nectar and it was fascinating to watch Gouldie flit from one flower to another, prospecting. We could not decide which was more beautiful, the purple orchid or the Violet-Eared Hummingbird, but they certainly complemented each other.

For those who want to build in a number of cages as permanent fixtures, it is desirable to construct them so that with dividers

*Maturing baby blue budgie
(bars are starting to disappear).*

instead of tops, bottoms, and ends, they can be expanded or contracted as needed. This can be done by cutting sliding partitions of the metal netting, but I prefer to use ⅛-inch hardboard, not only for bottoms, but also for ends. If the vertical partitions are of wire the birds tend to land on them, and after a while this frays the tails. Solid dividers avoid this.

A large cage can be converted into a set of four by making the front into four parts, each with a door, and half-inch slots separating the four parts. Where the four corners come together at the center the four fronts can be made solid by a metal plate in the form of a four-leaf clover, with the dividers sliding in the slots between the "leaves." I have seen a unit of 24 cages built in this fashion that makes a single cage six feet tall and twenty-two feet wide when all the dividers are removed.

In recent years a new type of metal netting has come on the market that makes much nicer cages than the older hardware cloth. The latter is square mesh, but the newer style has rectangular holes. The most popular size for most fanciers is the ½ inch x 2 inch, which does quite well for all but the smallest waxbills. When painted flat black it looks very nice. There are various sizes of mesh and one

Mature blue budgie.

can pick one to suit his needs. I had a most satisfactory cage made for a macaw out of 1 inch x 2 inch size, and it looked lovely, although it would have worked just as well if the mesh had been larger.

For indoor cages it is often a good idea to have a metal shop make the tray to fit the need. If the tray is deep enough, it will prevent seed husks from flying out into the room, and when sprayed with a decorator's color to match the room, it can be made an integral part of the decor.

One of the problems faced by birds kept inside all the time is the artificial schedule they are forced to keep. In the natural state they get up at dawn and retire at dusk. In our living rooms they are more likely to retire after the late, late show. It is not essential, but it is better for the birds if they are in a part of the room where they can settle down when they want to. Absence of sunlight is a problem that can be remedied by putting Vitamin C in the food or using a sunlamp for a few minutes a day. I have never found either of these precautions necessary, but some fanciers feel that they are.

Aviaries

The ultimate dream of most fanciers sooner or later gets around to visions of a large walk-in aviary in the garden, filled with lush flowers and colorful, singing birds. Most of us are realistic enough to settle for whatever portion of that dream is possible, and scale it down to fit our circumstances.

It is neither difficult nor expensive to set up an outdoor aviary. The initial cost can be kept reasonably low, and the size and shape can be adjusted to the space available. A saw, hammer, and pair of tinsnips will suffice as tools for constructing a simple aviary, and the birds are not in the least insulted if the finished product does not look as though a professional carpenter had made it.

I live in central Indiana, where winters are rigorous. We have freezing rainstorms, subzero cold, and blizzards for three or four months a year, so it is the better part of wisdom for me to plan my outdoor flights for use only from May to October. If I lived in northern Canada, I probably would not bother with outside aviaries at all. And if a kind destiny ever permits me to settle permanently in southern Florida or California, I probably will have outdoor flights covering more square footage than the house I live in. What I am trying to say is that the outside flights should be built with ample study of their practical use. If your storms tend to come from the west, you should put the flight just east of some sheltering structure. If your problem is the merciless Arizona sun, build the aviary in the afternoon shadow of a high house or tree. If you live on a highway curve, place the flight so automobile headlights will not be a problem to the roosting birds. The first night for a new bird to face flashing lights could result in terror and chaos for the entire collection. Fear spreads through a flock quickly. If a neighbor loves cats as passionately as you do birds, it will be wise to keep as much of a buffer zone as you can between your interests; otherwise your hobby will be swallowed up by his!

In any case, it is wise to provide shelter from the weather. The simplest form of this is a sheet of heavy plastic or hardboard placed across the top at one end of the walk-in flight, and perhaps running down the end a foot or two from the top. Some fanciers replace the wire netting of the top and sides at one end of the aviary with wood, which provides open space but completely sheltered. These should all be placed at the end of the aviary that heads into the face of most storms.

Another approach to outside aviaries that has been very successful is the shelterbox, which provides an enlarged birdhouse accommodation. The box is usually about four feet cubed, with an entrance hole going to the flight. It ordinarily has a large window or glass door that can be opened for cleaning purposes and a small door at floor level for placing food and water in the box, both openings at the end of the box opposite the flight. The top of the box must be flush with the top of the aviary, or even a little higher, if possible. Most birds prefer to roost in the highest places and if the perches in the box are higher than those in the flight the birds are much more likely to spend nights in the shelterbox.

One of the ways to encourage the birds to use the box is to place the feed there. This has the added advantages of avoiding fright-

Breeding lutino budgie hen (note brown cere).

Yellow-Winged Sugarbird (male).

Napoleon Weaver (male in full color).

ening the birds in the flight, and the food is protected from the weather. A major disadvantage is the ease with which a bully can monopolize the box, starving the rest of the birds.

The most satisfactory of all outside aviary structures is one with a full-size shelter. This is a small building at least as tall as the flight and it provides ample space for the birds even when the weather keeps them indoors. During northern winters there may be weeks at a time when the birds cannot be let out, and a cozy house will keep them healthy and happy. Most common species of cagebirds can go through a northern winter in an unheated room of this kind if it is draft-free and water is available daily, rather than a dishful of ice. It is remarkable how adaptable to cold most birds are. I have had unheated closed flights with baby Zebra Finches when the temperature did not go above zero for two weeks at a time. But it is very important that there be no drafts. Cold they can take; drafts they cannot. And water twice daily is important when the room is below freezing.

There are two schools of thought regarding what goes into an outside flight other than birds. For ease of upkeep a concrete floor is simplest. When it becomes soiled one merely hoses it clean with a garden hose, and it is rat-proof.

More attractive esthetically is a planted aviary, but this requires more attention, although if it is not overpopulated with birds, it is not a serious problem. Your own tastes and the climate will determine the kinds of plants you place in it, but it is wise to avoid vines that will climb the netting and hide escape holes or obscure your view of the birds. If you expect to have breeding pairs it will be important that they not be disturbed during the summer by your having to prune a fast-growing shrub that never should have been planted in the enclosure in the first place.

The planted aviary makes for a much more natural setting and the birds look more attractive, especially if the species selected are the kinds that do not hide from sight in the foliage. But in the process of re-creating nature you also invite some of nature's pests. One of these is vermin, and the hiding places of a planted aviary may set off a population explosion of four-legged intruders.

Mice are at best a nuisance, at worst a threat to birdlife. If an aviary has a family of mice in it, there may be birds disturbed at night that beat themselves to death in terrified, blind flight when mice come onto the perch or into the nest. Mice's droppings are poisonous and should be kept out of the feed at all costs. It is a good idea to hang the feeding vessel from a wire that is passed through a funnel halfway up, or to place the feed on a mouse-proof table made by nailing a metal baking pan upside down on a stake, so mice can climb the stake but cannot get up onto the table created by the inverted pan.

I am sure it is not scientifically sound, but the evidence points to the proposition that mice multiply by spontaneous combustion. You can have no opening wide enough to slip a table knife into when, presto, mice will appear as if by magic. I am tempted to believe some of the feed merchants are smuggling mouse-seeds into the mixtures and they germinate after I put the seed into the hoppers. But whatever the source, mice are almost beyond avoiding, and constant vigilance is required. Tiny babies can squeeze through small mesh wire and once inside they thrive on the constant food supply, soon growing to where they could not leave through that same hole even if they wanted to.

Rats, weasels, and other vermin may become more of a problem. They can dig at a phenomenal rate and it is wise in constructing a planted aviary to place a barrier about fifteen inches into the ground under the aviary. The simplest way is to pour a concrete foundation about that depth, then mount a 2 × 4 on top of it as the bottom support for the frame to hold the wire netting. Instead of this some fanciers dig a trench a foot deep and two feet wide around the aviary, running the wire netting down below ground level, then flared outward across the bottom of the trench so a digging animal will not be able to dig straight down to get under the wire.

Marauding dogs can be kept out of a yard by an adequate fence, but cats are only challenged by it. To keep cats, rats, and other vermin out of the yard a dog of your own may be the answer, but if you are trying to breed temperamental pairs of birds, a noisy dog may be almost as annoying to the birds as a cat that prowls on the roof of the flight. To solve this need some fanciers are keeping the African barkless dog, the Basenji. This breed makes a wonderful family pet. I speak from experience. A Basenji is a little taller than a beagle, has erect ears, curled tail, and a deeply furrowed brow. His alert manner, longish neck, and long legs give him the nickname of "little deer." All the Basenjis we have had have been very gentle around children, unusually intelligent, quick to learn that birds must not be molested, and—best of all—silent. The Basenji cannot bark. Other than an occasional loveable soft croon of delight the only sound ours has made comes at noon on Saturday, when

Mature normal green budgie.

the Civil Defense siren is blown for testing, and the sound apparently stirs something primeval in the Basenji and he howls with a cracked, unused voice from the depths of his being.

I have heard that some fanciers have found geese to be effective deterrents against cats, too, although I have never tried them. I can readily imagine that a hissing gander would throw a scare into a cat that would propel him over the fence in a hurry.

The constant threat with outside aviaries is escaping birds. I think there is no frustration in the life of the aviculturist more painful than having to stand helplessly in the doorway as a treasured

Green Cardinal (male).

bird soars up into the sky. Some species have a fantastic ability to spot an opening.

There are two ways to reduce escapes through open doors. The best is to build a small vestibule so the person entering can close a door behind him before he opens the one ahead. This is not difficult to construct. It can be done by building a diagonal wall across a corner of the flight, making a triangular vestibule large enough for one person.

A much simpler but also less secure arrangement is a low door into the flight, built so that you have to stoop to go through it. The reason this usually works is that birds will nearly always attempt to fly *over* any person who approaches them. If you have to stoop to enter through the door, the frightened birds will be circulating well above the opening.

And let this warning note be sounded: *never* build a doorway leading into a bird enclosure all the way to the ceiling. This invites escape. Always provide as much wall above the door as you can conveniently. And where possible the door should be on the side of the aviary from which disturbances usually come, because if someone runs up to the aviary from one side just when you are opening a door on the other side, it may be like shooing the birds out the open door.

When you are planning an aviary, you need to decide what kind of birds you intend to keep in it over a long period of time. I know people who put in one-inch mesh for larger birds and later regretted not having put in half-inch that would hold smaller birds. As a precaution you should use a smaller mesh if there is any question. You can use small mesh satisfactorily for large birds, but the reverse is not possible.

After years of experience I have come to the point where I use only lightweight (22-gauge) three-eighths-inch hexagon poultry-type netting in constructing either outside flights or inside cages. This holds the smallest possible bird; yet the wire itself is fine enough that it gives good visibility, especially when covered with flat black paint. This kind of wire mesh is made only in Japan and Germany, but it is available from importers here and is no more expensive than other forms of netting. Its one inconvenience is in its fragility under the rapacious hooked beak of a parrot-family member, so when I have to cage any psittacine bird larger than a lovebird I put a layer of heavier netting on the inside of the 2 × 2 framework, thereby making a double thickness of wire netting, the inside heavy and the outside light, with a two-inch space between.

This double protection comes in handy in other situations as well. When small birds are caged next to carnivorous larger birds it may be suicide for the smaller to land on the wire. I have a crippled Zebra Finch now who made the mistake of getting too close to an Indian Tree Pie, which is a form of magpie, that tried to pull him through the wire with gluttonous intent. Breeders of parrots frequently double-wire their partitions between flights to reduce the incidence of missing toes. A macaw can amputate another's toe with one quick slash, but not if the partition consists of two layers of wire separated by a 2 × 4 frame.

As was noted in the chapter on hookbills, it is necessary to protect wood from their ambitious beaks. A moderately active bird can go through a 2 × 2 post in an afternoon without difficulty. Therefore it is necessary to put the heavy wire netting inside the frame rather than outside, which makes it look like a halloween ghost with his skeleton on the outside. For large cockatoos it is best to use cyclone-fence if possible. For other large hookbills heavy welded wire fabric of 12 gauge or thicker is preferable to galvanized hardware cloth because the latter contains lead beads at the joints and a hookbill bird may tease at them until they become loose, then swallow them. A few years ago I had a very valuable macaw die in this unnecessary manner.

For serviceability the best kind of light wire to buy is galvanized after weaving. The initial cost is a bit more, but it is still less than hardware cloth would be. You can tell by checking the joints; if the twisted joints look as if they had been soldered, the wire is galvanized after welding. If they can be untwisted easily, they are obviously just some wires that are twisted around each other; they are galvanized before weaving and are less durable.

The netting that is galvanized after weaving will last for decades, even in rigorous climates. I am assured by experts that it can be buried for fifteen years and will still be intact, so it is good for running into the ground around the aviary for effective vermin-proofing.

For birds with less powerful beaks lighter wire netting is adequate. The hexagon poultry-netting type is strong enough for most purposes, but it breaks under stress and it does rust out after a few years. For that reason many fanciers prefer square-mesh hardware cloth. The main objection to hardware cloth (other than cost) is its visibility. The heavy galvanized wire reflects light and makes it hard to see through the wire. This problem can be re-

Red-Vented Bulbul.

duced by covering the wire with flat black paint, and I always do this to any wire netting I put anywhere. It is simplest to paint the wire flat on the floor, so I spread out newspapers, unroll a long piece of netting, and paint it before I cut it to fit the space for which it is intended.

If you are building outside aviaries for breeding rather than for a mixed collection you will want to make the flights a different proportion, probably. In any cage or aviary length is much more important than width. A bird gets his exercise by flying from one end to the other rather than from side to side. In breeding all but the colony-type finches (Zebras, Silverbills, etc.) it is much bet-

Red-Billed Weaver (foreground) and Black-Headed Weaver.

ter to have pairs alone in their flights and an aviary 3 feet wide by 6 feet high by 6 feet long is large enough for a pair of almost any hardbill or softbill you would want to breed. Flights for larger hookbills are usually about twice as wide and three times as long.

I have found that having a water outlet in or near an aviary is a great convenience. On hot summer days fresh drinking water is appreciated in the afternoon, and a fine spray of water from a sprinkler will put the birds in ecstasy. A stream of water from the hose will also simplify the cleaning chores.

Perhaps a word of caution should be said about the use of paint.

Any paint with lead content ought to be avoided around birds or animals. Even species that do not ordinarily chew the woodwork may on occasion do so, and the lead content (which is in most of the more expensive paints) may produce lead poisoning. This is especially important around parrot-family birds because of their chewing habits.

As a general rule I prefer to varnish or stain the wood I use, whether in framework or nestboxes, but when paint is required, I get non-toxic paint and use no other, even for painting buildings where there may be an outside flight added years later. The last I got was called "Ranch White" by the manufacturer, and it was made specifically for farm use. Leadless paint may have to be replaced sooner than lead-content paint, but I would rather replace the paint than the birds.

The label on the can ordinarily indicates whether lead is present. If it says that there is no lead content, that it is non-toxic, or that it can be used on babies' furniture, then it is safe.

Most of what has been said in this section on aviaries has assumed that they are outside. However, there are many fanciers with inside aviaries that are very satisfactory. Interior designers are picking up the beauty of a natural setting and are using planted indoor aviaries with great effectiveness. I have seen restaurants and professional reception areas with this treatment, as well as several lovely homes. In general, indoor aviaries are planned with the same factors in mind as for outdoor aviaries, except that sanitation is sometimes a bit more awkward and one should avoid ledges on which droppings may create a problem. Overcrowding indoors is more of a problem, and softbills in particular may create an odor problem if too many of them are placed in an indoor aviary constructed so that it is difficult to clean the corners. I have been told that some fanciers have used the newly marketed deodorizing kitty litter with success, but I have had no personal experience with it.

Feeding

Like people, birds develop individual tastes. Sometimes two birds of the same species will show quite different preferences in diet, and there are times when a bird will go very hungry rather than take a food that you have been giving regularly to another bird of the same species.

Unlike people, birds do not appreciate a frequent change of fare. Regardless of how well he likes beans, a male human does not want them thirty days in a row. But most birds prefer to stick pretty much to the same diet indefinitely. Strange foods should be introduced in small amounts and with care that the bird is not starving rather than to eat the new concoction.

As far as food is concerned, there are three basic types of birds: hardbills, softbills, and nectarines. Although there may be some overlapping in the foods they eat, each of them presents a different set of dietary needs. I have tried to be specific in the earlier chapters where individual species are discussed. This section will be more general.

Hardbills and Hookbills

Hardbills are seedeaters, and although the percentage may vary, most of their food comes in seed form. Some of them will not touch fruit or insects, while others require such supplements.

There are four basic seeds used in feeding cagebirds: millet, rape, canary, and sunflower. In addition to these there are scores of seeds running from tiny radish to large peanut, but most mixtures are composed primarily of one or more of the four basics.

Millet comes in several varieties. The small yellow form is sold under various names but is most frequently called finch millet or panicum. It is quite small, perfectly round, yellow, and rather cheap. Small finches, waxbills, etc., can get along adequately on this millet and nothing else.

The large millet is usually called proso millet and is the main ingredient in mixtures for budgies and larger finches, but it also is used commercially as a livestock feed, notably for pigs. It is large, perfectly round, yellow or white, and is very cheap.

Spray millet is seed still on the stalk, with thousands of tiny, round, brownish seeds still embedded in the flower head, which is from six to twelve inches in length. This is the most expensive way to feed millet, but the birds seem to enjoy it the most.

There is also a red millet that is about midway in size between

*Tri-Colored Nun (left) and Black-Headed Nun.
(Note that both birds have overgrown toenails—
a common problem with all nuns.)*

the small and the large. It is a bright rust color and has a small rib that keeps it from being perfectly round. Some finches are especially fond of it and it is usually found in finch and budgie mixtures. Similar to red millet in size is the perfectly round, black rape, the second most numerous seed found in canary mixtures. Its cost is slightly higher than that of red millet.

Canary seed, as distinguished from canary feed mixture, is an important ingredient in most mixtures. Canary is a flat, oval, grayish-yellow seed and is rather costly, about double the price of panicum millet. Most hardbill birds like it, and it is found in most mixtures, but because it is more expensive than many other seeds, the cheaper the mixture is, the less the percentage of canary.

For large parrot-family species sunflower is the basic food. It is highly nutritive, and the birds do adequately on it alone for a while, although they ought to have a parrot mixture, which usually contains a little hemp, millet, corn, oats, pepper pods, and peanuts.

In addition to the dry seeds discussed here, many of the hardbills and hookbills like fruit, vegetable, and live food. The appropriate discussion of the species should be checked to verify the diet needed.

SOFTBILLS

The softbills are a varied group. In general they eat a lot of fruit and/or live food. Fortunately it is possible to purchase their food in convenient form now, and their care is not difficult. Softbills tend to become tame much more quickly than most hardbills, and it is especially gratifying to have one fly to meet you for a tidbit whenever you come in sight.

There are several good mixtures for softbills on the market. Some is sold as "insectivorous mixture," some as "mynah food," and some as "mockingbird food." Content varies considerably, and when you find a mixture your birds seem to like, you ought to stick with it. Most brands are somewhat subject to age and ought to be kept closed and in a cool place if they are to be stored for a period of time. It is possible to buy the separate ingredients and mix your own, but this is a messy task and not worth the trouble to me.

In addition to this basic mixture, most softbills require a good supply of fruit daily, especially oranges, bananas, apples, and grapes. The oranges should be sliced across the grain so the fleshy meat is exposed and not the tough dividers of the segments. I usually cut an orange into thirds and when I come back it is picked clean as can be, just the rind remaining. The leftover peelings of fruit and uneaten portions can be rinsed and tossed in the mealworm bin.

Most softbills need a few mealworms each day. Mealworms are the larval stage of a darkling beetle (*Tenebrio molitor*), and they are easily raised. Start with a few beetles (or mealworms, if you do not have beetles yet) in a tub with four inches of cereal meal in the bottom. The cereal can be bought inexpensively at any grain elevator or farm supply store. The start of mealworms can be bought at a pet shop or fish bait store. They require no care, except for an occasional piece of fruit rind or similar moist vegetable matter (potato peelings are fine) as food and moisture. In about three months the crop matures; you will have thousands of mealworms. And if you prefer to buy them instead of raising them you can get them at quantity prices through bird magazine ads.

Other forms of live food can be caught outside. Grasshoppers, spiders, etc., are choice morsels relished by most softbills. There are funnel-shaped screen traps on the market that catch insects in large numbers. A small light in the shrubs of an outdoor planted aviary will attract a host of insects during the night that will hide in the bushes and still be there the next day for the inquisitive birds to find. But keep the bulb small so the birds will not be restless.

Some zoos have found that the easiest live food to raise is cockroaches. We all have a repulsion that blocks our use of this form, perhaps, but they are easy to raise, they are very nourishing, and the birds love them.

To provide small insectivorous birds with live food is fairly easy. Expose overripe banana or orange to the air for a couple of days, and it will soon be a fruit-fly culture. If the appearance offends you, put it in a plastic cup with a hole in the top after it is producing flies, and as they escape through the hole they will be snapped up in midair. Start another culture about every fifth day to keep the supply continuous.

NECTARINES

In many ways the most fascinating birds in the entire field of aviculture are the nectar-eaters, but since we have dealt with only a couple in this book, it may not be appropriate to dwell on the nectarines' dietary needs too much. The species we have discussed tend not to be purely nectarine, using nectar only as one part of the menu. The lorikeet eats considerable fruit and can, indeed, survive without any nectar at all for some period of time. The simplest nectar solution is made with honey and water or with sugar and water. These have two distinct advantages. They are very easily mixed, and neither gets sour within 24 hours except in very hot weather. It is obvious that these solutions offer a limited assortment of nutrients and are not in themselves sufficient for a complete diet over an extended period of time for any bird. A more complete diet, well balanced and quite sufficient for all nectar-eaters, even those subsisting on nectar alone, is the formula developed by Capricorn Aviaries of New York City, the country's leading hummingbird specialists. Following is an excerpt from their publication, "Notes on Hummingbirds."

CAPRICORN uses an altered version of the Lasiewski Formula. A full discussion of Dr. Lasiewski's work with hummers may be found in the *Avicultural Magazine* (British), Vol. No. 68, March/April issue, 1962.
Our version of this formula is as follows:
½ cup of plain granulated sugar
1½ tsp. of Mellin's Food
1½ tsp. of Gevral
3 tsps. of evaporated milk
8 drops of Vipents Multivitamins
6 drops of *Linatone*
Add water to make one pint of liquid. Mix thoroughly with egg-beater or food blender. Teaspoon measurements are the regulated plastic spoons used in food preparation, level not heaping. The mixture may be refrigerated but should be re-stirred with each use, for the powdered ingredients settle to the bottom in time.

Although I have not had experience with it personally I have been told that some are having success with a Metrecal solution. It was developed originally as a dietary supplement for people who were not getting adequate nutritive value out of their food intake. Its use in reducing diets was later recommended because it contains a wide assortment of many nutrients in proper balance. While birds' needs and humans' needs vary, perhaps both are met in large part by Metrecal. I think I would add not only water but also sugar to fortify it with readily burned fuel for nectarines. You may feel a little self-conscious about buying an armload of Metrecal. Take my advice and do not try to convince the druggist that it is for the birds. He will be sure your problem is bats.

The Capricorn formula is intended for daytime use. At the close of the day unused nectar should be removed. For birds subsisting on nectar alone it is customary to keep a sugar-water solution before them at night. As soon as hummingbirds awaken in the morning they need food, and the sugar-water nectar remains sweet overnight. For lorikeets this precaution is not necessary.

6

When Illness Comes

I N NO OTHER AREA is it more true that prevention is most of the cure than with cagebirds. The rate of recovery among ailing cagebirds is discouragingly low, and if one can do anything to prevent illness, he may save fatal complications. Likewise, catching an illness while it is still developing increases the likelihood of cure tremendously. The experienced aviculturist glances over his charges daily, and his practiced eye will note a bird that is having difficulty. And while he is glancing over the birds he spots empty food hoppers, upset water dishes, a loose piece of string that could entangle a bird, a nestbox ajar so a bird might fall behind it, a break in the wire netting, lettuce in the water dish, mouse droppings in the seed, and any of a hundred other causes for alarm.

More than any other single cause of death that I have encountered over the years, I think, is a totally unnecessary one: neglect to be certain. A water font that has a ring around the inside may look as though it is half full but actually be empty. A glass-fronted feed hopper may be full of seed but impacted so none of the seed can fall out for the birds. An orange may have been cut the wrong way so the birds cannot get to the meat. One time I replaced four

119

pairs of Zebra Finches one after another in the home of a friend before I discovered that the birds were eating the seeds until the cup had a top layer of chaff, then would starve to death because my friend could see that the feed cup was full and would not disturb it.

I cannot say this too loudly: check all feed and water containers every day. And water is if anything more important than seed. Many birds cannot get along 24 hours without it. It is not necessary to give fresh food and water daily, but they must be checked.

Another general caution is in regard to placement of the food and water containers. They must be clear of any overhead perch, because droppings are a source of trouble. In an aviary or large cage for mixed collection it is a good idea to have food and water at two well-separated parts of the enclosure so a bully cannot starve other birds by keeping them from the dishes. Grit should be available at all times as well as food and water. It is very rare that a bird will overeat. Quantities do not need to be controlled, although sometimes certain kinds of food need to be reduced in the diet.

A sick bird almost always looks sick. He sits listlessly on the perch or floor, all feathers fluffed out, often with eyes that appear tiny (because surrounding feathers are disarranged), sometimes with his wings held out slightly from the body, and shivering. A bird that sits fluffed out, with *both* feet on the perch, and his head under his wing during the day probably needs immediate attention. Birds sometimes take a nap during the day, especially if the human family has kept them up late the night before, but they rarely do so with both feet on the perch.

Although several things can be done, the best and almost universal treatment is heat. I have more faith in the application of heat to a sick bird than any other remedy and often heat alone is all that is needed.

The patient should be placed in 85° to 90° F. and kept there for several hours—up to 24 hours, after which the temperature should be reduced gradually. Be in no hurry to restore him to his original cage. Take up to 48 hours to get him back to normal temperature if it has been a severe illness.

For fanciers who have only one or two birds a specially constructed hospital cage probably is not warranted. A 40-watt light bulb placed near a small cage, over both of which a covering has been placed (avoid fire) will serve as a make-shift hospital cage. Use a thermometer to check the temperature and keep it between 85° and 90° by adjusting the cover.

For those who have enough birds to justify it, a hospital cage can be purchased from firms dealing in supplies and equipment for exotic cagebirds, or one can be built easily. Make a box about 18″ high x 18″ wide x 12″ deep, leaving one of the largest sides uncovered. Put on the inside bottom three electric light sockets, each wired to a switch outside so any number of the 40-watt bulbs can be turned on at a time. A few inches above the bulbs put a metal floor, and about three inches above it a perch in such a position that food and water dishes will not be beneath it. Have glass cut to slide into channels formed by molding on the open side, and have the glass go down only to the metal floor. On the inside back wall hang a thermometer. Across the top have a slot about 1½″ x 18″ for ventilation, covered with wire netting.

When you have a sick bird you lift the glass slide (unless you have a cabinet-maker's skill and have installed a door) and put in water, feed, and the bird. Turn on one 40-watt bulb, then in a half hour another, then another if needed. Control the degrees of heat by the number of bulbs burning and, if needed, laying something over the hole at the top. But remember that the bird has to breathe.

If you are giving medicine also, you should use a small water container, and it should be convenient for the bird to drink from. After 24 hours of 85° to 90° the bird should be acting much better. If not, continue the heat another 12 to 24 hours. After he appears well, turn off one light, then a few hours later another, then another so that he adjusts slowly to the lowering temperature.

During the time he is in the hospital cage he probably will eat very little, but he should have an inviting assortment of whatever might tempt him. And the water dish must be watched because the water will evaporate quickly.

Antibiotics have come on the market recently and can be secured either from veterinarians or from pet shops. Usually they are given through the water and it is a good idea to give them whenever illness appears, in addition to the heat treatment.

Chills

Probably the commonest of all ailments among cagebirds is the chill. Most birds can take cool temperatures but none can take drafts, and a bird that is exposed to a draft, especially while roosting at night, is a prime candidate for the sick bay.

Symptoms for chill are the standard illness symptoms already described, and the treatment likewise. A bird that has recovered from a chill should be normal in every way within a short while and can be restored to his cage. If he has been outside and contracts the chill during winter weather, it is questionable wisdom to restore him to the outside flight until spring, however.

Enteritis

Probably second most common among bird ailments is the intestinal ailment called enteritis. Symptoms are similar to the general illness signs described, but they are usually attended by watery droppings and frequently by soiled feathers under the vent. This ailment is more difficult to treat than the chill and probably ought to have aureomycin or similar antibiotic treatment in addition to the heat. It sometimes is caused by soiled food, wilted greens, or some other form of contamination, and a bird with a serious case of enteritis is sick indeed.

Degenerative Ailments

This very ambiguous term covers a poorly defined group of illnesses. I am not at all sure what the veterinary diagnosis of "going light" is, but the symptoms are fairly well agreed on by aviculturists. Although the bird continues to eat normally—or sometimes even more than normally—he continues to lose weight. When you pick up such a bird, the feel is unmistakable. His breastbone, which ought to be hardly noticeable to a casual handling, sticks out like a knife. His breast muscles have degenerated and he weighs almost nothing. He feels like nothing but a handful of feathers. In the later stages of the disorder he does not have enough strength to fly to a perch, so he spends his time either at the feed dish or huddled in a corner. I know of no treatment for this illness and as far as I have been able to observe it, the ailment is irreversible. There is only one outcome.

I have always suspected that this is related to old age, too. Sometimes birds I have had for years will suddenly develop symptoms of "going light," but I have felt that in their cases it probably was just a case of the machinery wearing out, like a Model T Ford. Even the most persistent of them finally failed.

But "going light" is certainly not merely old age. I have had too many birds whose ages I knew to be young contract the disorder for me to think it is always senile degeneration.

Constipation

Although diarrhea is more common and is usually associated with enteritis, constipation does sometimes occur in cagebirds. The evidence is seen in a bird that squats and flicks his vent as if he were evacuating, but without success. He may develop a sluggish manner, too. Treatment ought to include greens or sprouted seed if he will take it, and heat if the case is severe. Some fanciers give two drops of cod-liver or mineral oil with success, but I have had no experience with this approach.

Eggbinding

One of the most dangerous of all ailments with cagebird hens is eggbinding. This ailment is related to but not restricted to cold weather. A hen that is trying to lay has to flex sets of abdominal muscles, and if cold or nervousness should upset them, she cannot pass the egg. This is a fatal condition if not relieved.

Three methods are commonly used. Some fanciers put a couple of drops of olive or vegetable oil directly in the vent with a cotton-tipped stick. Others hold the bird's vent over a pot of boiling water so this avian Turkish bath will relax her. I have tried both systems many times but have by far my best results from the heat of a regular hospital cage. Usually the hen deserts the nest and quits laying after a case of eggbinding, but not always.

An eggbound hen can be recognized by her general ill appearance. Often she will be on the floor, unable to fly to a perch. When examined you will find her abdomen extended and by feeling—be ever so gentle!—you can find the egg stuck in the channel. With some species you may not have known that she was the least interested in nesting, and even out-of-season eggbinding may occur. Indeed, it may be less common during breeding season because then the birds are prepared for the process, and other circumstances are favorable.

Broken Limbs

Occasionally a wing or leg will get broken. In smaller birds splints can be made of toothpicks and the leg held to them by Scotch tape. Wings can be reset and held in place by a snug jacket made of nylon hose sewn in place. In either case the bird should be in a small cage with no high perches to tempt him to use the wounded limb.

Larger birds can be treated the same way, using popsickle sticks for splints. Hookbill birds are difficult to treat because their powerful beaks can demolish any bandage in seconds.

If the bird is especially valuable to you, it may be wise to have a veterinarian set the limb. My experience with setting legs has been moderately successful, but getting a wing to mend perfectly is rare.

In cases where a foot or leg is mashed and amputation is necessary, a clean cut can be made with sharp scissors or nail clippers and the bleeding arrested in small birds with styptic powder from a drugstore. A veterinarian is a much better bet in such a case, though.

Foot and Beak Troubles

Some species seem to have more trouble than others with their feet. One of the best preventive measures is to use natural tree twigs instead of the nice new perches that come with cages or the usual perches consisting of dowels sold in lumberyards. Natural twigs are not so attractive as clean dowels, but they are better adapted to the needs of the birds in that their rough surfaces scrape the feet clean and their varied sizes exercise the foot muscles better. For chewing birds it is wise to use branches from fruit trees, berry bushes, eucalyptus trees, etc. Avoid pine trees and others that give off resin.

Baby budgies are probably the greatest sufferers of all from dirty feet. While in the nest their toes collect the moist droppings and each toe builds up a ball of hard excrement. I have seen crippled babies hardly able to walk because of large globs attached to the toes.

Removal of the balls must be done cautiously. The best way is to soak the foot, but this is tedious. I usually chip away at the ball gently with my thumb nail or a sharp knife. The temptation is to slide it off the toe, but after you take a toe nail with it once, you learn this is not the way to do it. The same problem sometimes develops with baby budgie's beaks when mother is a wet feeder.

Members of the Munia family (nuns, Spicebirds, etc.) for some reason I do not understand are prone to grow long curled nails in captivity. I have seen them coiled like a corkscrew and many times their normal length. Other species sometimes have this problem also, including canaries.

Aside from its ugliness, the overgrown nail is undesirable because birds become entangled in the wires of the cage or in crevices in perches. Prevention pays off and trimming the nail is simple.

It is important that the nail be trimmed beyond the blood vessel. By holding the nail up to a good light you can see where the blood vessel ends and with ordinary fingernail clippers snip off the part of the nail beyond the blood. The first few times you try it have a styptic pencil on hand—rob hubby's shaving kit for it—just in case you miss or the bird jumps at the wrong time.

In some birds the upper or lower beak may grow out of proportion to the other half. This makes feeding a difficult task and may actually starve the bird. In any case it becomes quite unsightly. If you can see the blood vessel as described above for the toe nail, use the same procedure. If not, trim the oversize beak back almost to where it was originally and to match the other half, and you probably will be safe.

Feather Trouble

Sometimes fanciers become frantic because suddenly they find bundles of feathers in the cage corners and wonder if the bird is ill. Usually he is not. Most birds moult heavily once or twice a year, and the feathers they drop may accumulate and cause alarm. As long as the bird is active and appears healthy, he probably is well. Singing birds tend to sing less while moulting. Canaries, for instance, are relatively quiet in early fall.

Some species go into eclipse plumage for a few months, during which they are extremely drab and colorless. Then in just a couple of weeks the males explode into the dazzling color of their nuptial plumage. Of the birds available here, the weavers are probably the commonest birds that go through this fascinating metamorphosis. But the change back to drabness comes, too, and what was once a gorgeous bird may come to look like a female English sparrow shortly. Be patient; after a few months of quiet and rest he will emerge again as a glowing example of how lavish nature can be with color.

Perhaps another cause for alarm should be met here. As has been indicated above, some Indian exporters have discovered that plain-colored birds that do not sell can be made into bright-colored birds that do sell by dipping them in dye. Thousands of gorgeous yellow, green, purple, or red birds are sold each month in this country, only to become drab female Strawberry Finches, Silverbills, Spicebirds, nuns or drab females of other varieties. When a bird of this kind moults out the bright color, he will never again recover it; it was dye on the old feathers and it is gone forever.

Bareness is another matter. A bird that is in a normal moult rarely has much bare flesh exposed. Nature works gradually and replaces feathers constantly. If the bird looks as though a bundle of feathers had been plucked out, it is probably because they have been. This is called "feather plucking" and is usually caused by another bird with an over-active beak, although occasionally a bird will do it to himself. Often the plucking is brought about by a desire to nest, but I am convinced that some birds do it out of sheer boredom, especially parrots.

If the bird being plucked is in with other birds, remove him and within two weeks he should look like new. The damage is rarely permanent. If you can identify the bird doing the plucking, remove him (or more frequently her) for a few weeks, then restore him. He should be over it. If the bird being plucked was alone, obviously plucking himself, give him another cage, change perches, give him toys, add Vitamin C, increase his greenfood, and do anything else you can think of to divert him from a bad habit.

There are some effective salves on the market, I understand, and you can get them in a fully stocked pet shop. A report from one bird fancier shows repeated success in restoring feathers through applying Elizabeth Arden's *8-Hour Cream*®.

Baby budgies are subject to a disorder called "French Moult," a disheartening malady that seems to strike without rhyme or reason. It occurs when they are about three or four weeks old, just before they leave the nest. A thousand theories have been spun and some scientific research has been conducted, but I think no one can explain the cause or cure fully yet.

Badly affected birds lose many of their body and wing feathers. Sometimes called "runners," they cannot fly because they do not have the wing feathers to support their body weight. They are usually weaklings. Although some outgrow their condition, most of them never completely recover. Some of the babies sold in stores as "tame" are really runners that never had wings with which to fly, but not all of them. If you see a lot of baby budgies in an open play pen in the store, check to see whether there are wing-feather stumps where scissors were used to cut the feathers. If not, chances are that they are French Moult runners that have not developed wing feathers, cannot fly, and therefore are "tame."

A pair of breeding budgies may have French Moult in this nest and not in the next. They may have one or two babies with it in this nest, or all of the babies. Heredity appears not to be the deciding factor, nor the kind of care the birds are getting. Some of the best fanciers in the world have it in their flock this year but not next year, although they have not changed a thing they are doing. It is a great mystery and there is little you can do about it.

Mites and Lice

Occasionally birds are bothered by mites or lice, though not often. They usually are not seriously damaging to adult birds, who seem to have enough strength to withstand the drain of energy by these parasites that suck their blood. Babies are not so fortunate, however, and especially canary and budgie babies are threatened by an invasion.

The fancier who suspects the presence of lice or mites can check easily by throwing a white cloth over the cage before the lights go out. After an hour in the dark, turn on the lights and the cloth will show tiny black or gray moving spots if there are parasites present. They hide in the cracks in the cage during the daytime but come out at night to feed on the inactive birds.

The red mite gets his name from his gorged state. Just after he has feasted he is full of red blood and shows up the color. In his more normal state he is a whitish gray and can be recognized as looking like a sprinkling of white pepper along the cracks of cages. Unless you look closely you do not see movement. He likes to hide under paper or elsewhere where he is not exposed.

There are effective sprays and powders on the market. I like to dip the entire cage in the solution if possible (in my wife's laundry tub if she is not looking!) and keep it immersed for several minutes.

Finches and birds other than canaries and budgies seem to be less threatened by these parasites. I do not understand why. Once they get a head start among canaries or budgies during breeding season, they can be difficult to deal with.

There is no disgrace in having them. You may have been extremely cautious and spotlessly clean with your birds, but if a starling or a sparrow lands on your windowsill he may leave the beginning of an invasion of your delectable birds, and you may not detect it until there are scores of thousands of the parasites in your cages.

Dizziness

Not a common ailment but one that does cause grave concern when it occurs is vertigo. The symptoms usually are a grotesque twisting of the head over the shoulder or throwing it straight up or even back so that the head is inverted and the crown is on the nape of the neck. The bird has little or no sense of balance and is unable to fly in a direct line. Sometimes this is accompanied by blindness.

Causes are varied. There appears to be a disturbance to the organs of equilibrium through accident or from another source. I have never found a successful treatment. A few of my birds with these symptoms have recovered spontaneously, but most of them die before long. The more severe cases I relieve of their misery.

7

On Buying Birds
and Other Useful Information

To AVOID DISTRESS later on a few simple but important precautions should be taken in buying birds.

Broken feathers are no great problem, and even a frayed tail is not serious. If the birds have been housed in such a way that they were encouraged to land on wire screen frequently—this happens in a long and narrow cage—tail feathers may be unsightly. They will grow back.

But never, never buy a bird that is soiled around the vent. This is likely a sign of disease and even if you get the bird free, you are taking home a Trojan horse. Avoid it like the plague, which, in fact, it may be.

Also avoid any bird that sits listlessly and fluffed out on the perch. Some species move little, like Amazon Parrots, but for any of the active species a dull bird is a poor risk. If it is puffed out and sleeping on both feet during the day, beware. This can be misleading, because some stores are open late every night and the birds are unable to get enough sleep unless they doze during the day. If it is not overdone, the birds are not seriously harmed by it, but any time you buy a bird that is sleeping during the day, you are inviting trouble.

Any bird that keeps its feathers fluffed out from the body is likewise showing a symptom usually associated with illness. I have supposed this is an effort to control fever or chill, but I am not positive that this is the reason. I am positive, however, that it usually indicates some type of disorder.

One of the problems that has come with the increasing popularity of cagebirds has been a shortage of people who know how to care for them and love them enough to give them considerate attention. Some outlets sell birds at such a low margin of profit that they have little leeway with which to give them the care they need. Notice the food and water dishes in the cages. If they are empty or soiled, it is likely that the birds on sale have also been neglected before, and it is probable that their resistance is lowered as a result of it. It is no bargain to buy a bird at half price if he will not survive long after you get him home. Birds are not expensive these days, and it is foolish and wasteful to save a couple of dollars if it means getting a substandard bird. If you do not know how to select a good bird, it is very important that you select a reliable dealer and trust him. He makes more money on the feed he will sell you than on the bird, so he wants it to live for a long time.

We have developed a specialized business of cagebird sales by mail in this country, and it runs on a surprisingly reliable basis. There are a few unscrupulous operators, as in every business, but they are uncommon. The shipping of birds requires experience and skill, and if you have a question about an advertiser, check back issues of the magazine. If he was advertising a year ago, you can probably rely on him. If you have a question, ask the editor of the magazine if he has had any complaints. You will get a direct answer.

The number of people importing exotic cagebirds is limited, and this is why you may not be able to find what you want in your home town. You can order with confidence from reputable importers if they guarantee live delivery. I know one who has shipped to all parts of the United States and Canada in the past few years and has not lost a bird enroute.

Birds are usually shipped by air, which is cheaper than rail, and except for shipments of hookbills (requiring larger and heavier cages), bird crates ordinarily go for the minimum fee. I live near the geographic center of the United States, and the cost of the average shipment of a half-dozen pairs of finches runs about five dollars to either coast.

Should there be difficulties on the arrival of the birds, fill out a "bad order" report from the transportation company and send it the same day to the shipper. Usually he will replace the birds and then debate with the transportation company about who was to blame.

Whether the birds are bought locally or by mail there are a few things you can do to ease their adjustment to their new home. If you are going to be putting them with other birds, they should be watched rather closely for a few days while they settle down. The birds already there have an established pecking order, that is, they know who bosses whom, and there is a minimum of fighting. A new bird in the flight is a threat to every old bird, and they have to place him in the hierarchy of power, which means a certain amount of bickering for a few days. Just be sure it does not become mayhem.

If it is a large flight, it is a good idea to place the feeding dishes in plain view where the new bird cannot avoid seeing them. Remember that the new cage is a new world to him, and he does not know his way around it. Be sure he is eating.

Like many people, birds resist strange foods. Just as you would become very hungry if you were suddenly transported to Africa and offered a diet consisting of native dishes of fried grasshoppers, rice soup, and water buffalo, so a new bird resists strange foods. It helps if he sees his cage mates eating what you offer, but it does not completely eliminate the problem. Offer him as large a variety as you can at least for the first few days while he is getting over his early adjustment period.

When you get a new bird, you should already know what his diet has been by asking the dealer. If you have the bird shipped, ask when you send the order for the dealer to tell you what he has been feeding. He will be glad to do so. The food in the carton should also give you an indication.

If you cannot determine precisely what he has been eating you probably can classify him into one of four major groups. Most finch-type birds are hardbills and to them should be offered a wide assortment of seeds. As a basic minimum I suggest canary, rape, and white millet; as many other types as you can get will be worthwhile.

Softbills are usually frugivorous, insectivorous, or semi-insectivorous and require a softbill mixture (sometimes called "mockingbird food" in stores); apple, orange, banana, grape; and mealworms. Later you will want to add and subtract foods, but that menu should get him started.

Nectarine birds require a balanced solution, but for the immediate need they can get along on honey and water. I usually mix about one-fourth honey in the water. It is important to replace this as soon as you can with the more balanced diet that the dealer was giving him, though.

The fourth category is hookbill, and it includes all the birds of the parrot family except lorikeets. The latter are nectarine and frugivorous; give lorikeets the fruit diet, plus bread moistened with milk and laced with honey. Budgies are no problem; give them what is sold in stores as "parrakeet mixture," consisting primarily of white millet and canary. All the other hookbills take sunflower seed. The smaller ones like lovebirds and Red-Rump Parrakeets also should have the budgie mixture. Larger ones appreciate peanuts, pepper pods, and other seeds found in parrot mixtures. All hookbills relish dry bread.

With all hardbills and hookbills I am cautious about giving greenfood, fruit, or vegetables the first few days. Travel sometimes leads to loose bowels and such food seems only to aggravate the condition.

It is important that all birds have plenty of fresh water at all times. They will want to bathe in it, so have the container no deeper than their legs so they will not slip in and drown in a strange dish.

Some fanciers like to give newly arrived birds antibiotic medicine to clear the system. Any well-stocked pet shop or a veterinarian can supply you with the tablets. There are several brands on the market, and as far as I know, one is as good as another to reduce the possibility of infection.

Keeping Wild Birds

Occasionally fanciers get a yen to cross their cagebirds with some of our own wild birds. This can be a costly yen if it is indulged. Nearly all the birds of this kind are protected by federal or state legislation, and penalties are stiff, involving from six months to two years in prison plus $500 to $2,000 fine. If you want an official list of federal prohibitions, write for "Birds Protected by Federal Law" from the Fish and Wildlife Service, U. S. Department of the Interior, Washington, D. C. 20240. It is free. The edition of the list before me as I write contains about 500 entries, including the American Goldfinch (commonly called the Wild Canary), the Virginia Cardinal (commonly called Red Bird), and the Mourning Dove, all of which tempt most of us. In addition, there may be state laws to restrict you, too. Write to the Conservation Department at your state capital for their list.

Cagebird Societies

Some of the richest hours in the life of a cagebird fancier can be the time spent in bird-talk with others who share the same interest. In most large cities and in all states there are clubs that meet monthly, as a rule, and put on formal and informal programs of interest. You get a great deal of joy and learn a lot from them. Old-timers share their experiences and newcomers always have ideas to try out. At most club meetings some members bring birds that furnish a focus for special discussions, and there is usually an annual show where there may be hundreds of birds competing for ribbons and trophies. It is at the annual show that you find out how your birds compare with others. There are few thrills to match the one that comes when you find that the baby you cared for from the egg stage has won a trophy.

It is impractical to list the various state or local clubs here since the officers change so often, but a current list can be secured from the list published in *American Cage-Bird Magazine,* or from the editor.

There are national clubs, also, and they are a source of constant help to the fancier. They usually publish a bulletin that is full of information about the bird in which they specialize and ads tell you where to buy or sell birds. The following is a list of national and international clubs of general interest, but it is not a complete one. If you have a special interest not listed below, contact the editor of the *American Cage-Bird Magazine* for information. Most of the following have ads in the magazine from which you can get current secretaries' addresses; if not, the editor will gladly furnish them for you.

American Association of Roller Canary Breeders
American Budgerigar Society
American Border Fancy Canary Club
American National Roller Canary Association
American Singers Club
Avicultural Society of America
Bengalese Society (international club with offices in England; also called Society Finch)
International Border Fancy Canary Club
National Cage-Bird Exposition (sponsors annual show)
United Budgerigar Society
United States Association Roller Canary Culturists
Yorkshire Canary Club of America
Zebra Finch Society (international club with offices in England)

Other than the publications of the specialty clubs listed here there is only one commercial American periodical that regularly publishes material of interest to cagebird fanciers. It is devoted exclusively to cagebirds and consists of around fifty pages of articles, pictures, news, and advertisements. It has a monthly column entitled "Exotic Cage-Birds" which I have been writing since 1957. It is the only American publication that deals with all kinds of cagebirds and only with cagebirds. It is:

American Cage-Bird Magazine
3449 North Western Avenue
Chicago, Illinois 60618

A Closing Word

A number of years ago while I was a university student my wife and I lived in an apartment where pets were not permitted, but we thought there could be no objection to a small aquarium. On a hot summer evening we went to a tropical fish dealer's shop in downtown Chicago and I drooled over the gorgeous specimens he exhibited. My wife went to the cool, open doorway to wait for me and the owner stood nearby talking to her. This was at the time the discus fish was new and expensive. I came to the front of the shop to ask the price and when he said, "Fifty dollars each," I gasped. My wife exclaimed, "Anyone who would pay fifty dollars for a fish is stupid!"

The owner turned to her and said, "Lady, sit down in that chair!" When she had done so, he pointed his finger in her face, shook it emphatically, and said with kindness undergirded with an intense urgency, "Don't ever say that again. You should thank God your husband puts his money into something of beauty to have in his own living room. Just think how many men are pushing their money into a bartender's hands at the corner tavern instead of sitting at home in their living rooms, and be deeply thankful that your husband shows such good judgment!"

I have often thought of that fifteen-second sermon as one of the most significant ones I have ever heard. Over the years I have sold many birds for much more than fifty dollars each, and have bought a few, but I never fail to be just a little more appreciative of the significance when I recall the wise philosopher in the fish shop doorway.

Let more and more people find the satisfactions of home enriched and deepened by the feathered addition as they make room in their homes for a thing of beauty that spreads joy to all who see and hear.

Index

Page numbers in **boldface** indicate photographs